EWAN
MCGREGOR

BILLY ADAMS IS A FREELANCE JOURNALIST AND WRITER.
HE WORKED FOR HONG KONG'S TWO BIGGEST
ENGLISH-SPEAKING DAILY NEWSPAPERS, *THE SOUTH
CHINA MORNING POST* AND THE *EASTERN EXPRESS*, AS
WELL AS IN SYDNEY, AUSTRALIA, BEFORE RETURNING
TO SCOTLAND IN 1995. HE HAS WRITTEN ON A WIDE
RANGE OF SUBJECTS, MOST RECENTLY FOR SCOTLAND'S
BEST-SELLING DAILY NEWSPAPER, *THE DAILY RECORD*.
AT THE END OF 1997 HE LEFT THE *RECORD* TO WRITE
EWAN MCGREGOR. BILLY ADAMS LIVES IN EDINBURGH.

BILLY ADAMS

EWAN

MCGREGOR

THE
UNAUTHORISED
BIOGRAPHY

First published 1998
by B&W Publishing Ltd
Edinburgh

ISBN 1 873631 80 4

British Library Cataloguing in Publication Data:
A catalogue record for this book is available from
the British Library

Cover photograph by Adrian Green.
Courtesy of SHOOT.

Design: Winfortune & Associates

Printed by WSOY

ACKNOWLEDGEMENTS

TO THE LARGE NUMBER OF PEOPLE WHO HELPED AND CO-OPERATED
WITH MY RESEARCH FOR THIS BOOK, I OFFER MY SINCEREST THANKS.
WITHOUT THEIR ASSISTANCE IT WOULD NOT HAVE BEEN POSSIBLE.
I'M PARTICULARLY GRATEFUL TO THE FRIENDS AND COLLEAGUES OF
EWAN MCGREGOR WHO OFTEN SPOKE TO ME AT GREAT LENGTH,
ALBEIT SOMETIMES ON AN ANONYMOUS BASIS.

I WOULD LIKE TO THANK THE STAFF AT THE INFORMATION
DEPARTMENT OF THE BRITISH FILM INSTITUTE, AND AM DEEPLY
GRATEFUL TO THE SCOTTISH DAILY RECORD'S PICTURE EDITOR
STUART NICOL FOR HIS HELP IN THE COMPILATION OF THE
BOOK'S PHOTO SECTIONS.

THANKS TO ALYSE POZZO, CREATOR OF THE EXCELLENT UNOFFICIAL
EWAN MCGREGOR WEB SITE, FOR ALL HER HELP.

I ALSO WANT TO THANK ALISON MCBRIDE, PLUS CAMPBELL BROWN,
STEVE WIGGINS AND SIMON CAVE AT B&W FOR THEIR HELP AND
ADVICE. FINALLY, SPECIAL THANKS TO THOSE WHO KNOW ME BEST
FOR THEIR PATIENCE AND SUPPORT.

CONTENTS

PROLOGUE

CAN YOU FEEL THE FORCE?

This was it, the moment they had been waiting for—the Death Star looming into view, massive, filling the screen ahead. To Luke Skywalker and the other rebel pilots it seemed awesome, impregnable. Any attempt to get closer would surely be suicide. But this was no time for self-preservation, no time for doubt. If they failed now, the war against the Empire would be lost, and the rebels would be wiped out.

The enemy fire intensified, both from the gigantic fortress ahead and from the imperial fighters close behind. As the rebels closed in for the kill, the boy's mind, his whole being, was narrowed to a single thought—the Death Star must be destroyed. One shot, fired with pinpoint accuracy, would be enough. His body tensed and he gripped the arms of his seat as the target approached.

Suddenly a swarm of imperial fighters, led by Darth Vader himself, latched on to the tail of the two leading rebel craft. The rebels were hurtling along the narrow corridor towards their goal, but Vader was closing in relentlessly. He knew that if just one of these ships got through, it would all be over. They had to be stopped, whatever the cost.

With death closing in on him from astern, Skywalker was rapidly nearing his firing-point, emptying his mind of everything else. The boy could see the danger, he wanted to shout a warning. If Luke didn't see Vader soon . . .

Just at that moment one of the fighters in Vader's force disintegrated in a shower of flame. Another pilot panicked, swerving off course and scattering the rest of the pack, as an unseen attacker tore into them. In the confusion the boy caught a fleeting glimpse of Vader's craft, careering out of control into deep space. Then he recognised the attacker—it was Han Solo, in the *Millennium Falcon*. Skywalker had been saved by the man who had walked out on him.

Nothing could stop him now. With the voice of Obi-Wan Kenobi echoing in his mind, Skywalker disengaged his computer mask. The Force would guide him.

An instant later, he pressed the fire-control.

On the bridge of the Death Star, a distant rumble heralded the end. As the noise grew louder, time stood still for the crew. A devastating blow had been struck right at the heart of the Star, and they knew that in a few seconds the shock wave would tear their vast fortress apart.

The boy watched transfixed as the screen erupted and the Death Star was consumed in a blinding flash. The cinema audience reeled from the tremendous explosion, their faces picked out in stark relief by the intense white light from the screen. As the boy looked around the cinema, everyone was smiling, some were cheering. Against all the odds, Skywalker had triumphed.

Relief flooded over the audience as the film came to an end. The boy was overwhelmed by what he had witnessed. He had been anticipating this for months, had waited impatiently outside the school gates that day for his mother to drive him the 15 miles to the cinema. And now it was over.

Almost. There was one more thing. As the credits rolled, the boy strained to catch sight of a name—a familiar name. Finally, it appeared, in minuscule type: "Dennis Lawson". This was what really made *Star Wars* special. Lawson, who played one of the rebel pilots, was his uncle.

But as he sat there in the darkness of the cinema, the seven-year-old Ewan McGregor could never have imagined that, one day, he too would be part of the *Star Wars* legend.

I

THE MCGREGORS OF CRIEFF

On the edge of the Scottish Highlands lies the town of Crieff, a pleasant interlude for those on the road to the better-known tourist attractions of the North. But Crieff has not always been so tranquil—300 years ago it was the scene of the bloody exploits of Rob Roy MacGregor and his clan, and was considered to be one of the most violent towns in Europe. Crieff was renowned as a place where Highlanders would come together with those from the Lowlands to settle their differences—by fair means or foul. In those brutal times, the authorities showed little mercy to lawbreakers, wherever they came from, and many troublemakers ended their days swinging from the local gallows.

It was here that Ewan McGregor spent his childhood—although the town he grew up in was a different place altogether from the one which had witnessed the adventures of his roguish namesake Rob Roy. Crieff had long since abandoned its wild ways to become a haven for elderly tourists and day trippers.

Ewan Gordon McGregor arrived on the stage of life just after eight o'clock on the night of March 31, 1971. He was born in Perth Royal Infirmary, a hospital 15 miles from his home town. He was the second son of James Charles Stewart McGregor and Carol Diane McGregor. Theirs was a classic story of childhood sweethearts who fell in love among the textbooks at school in Crieff. The relationship eventually blossomed into marriage on a hot July day in 1966 at the town's St Michael's Parish Church.

At the ages of 23 and 21 respectively, both started work as schoolteachers, and in February 1969, when the couple were living in a flat in Glasgow's Edgemont Street, Carol and Jim celebrated the birth of their first son, Colin, at the city's Royal Maternity Hospital.

Work commitments soon brought them back to the town where they had met, when Carol started a job at the state-run Crieff Primary School, and Jim returned to their old school, the independent Morrison's Academy, as a physical education teacher.

Jim also became an active member of the local community. At Morrison's he advised the pupils on their careers, and ran the school cricket team. Outside, he was chairman of the local Round Table, and was on the organising committee of the annual Highland Games, at which he also commentated. Local historian Colin Mayell remembers that in 1973 Jim founded the town's rugby club, and became its captain. It is also interesting to note that Jim and Carol were among the founder members of the Crieff Film Society, set up in the seventies by a small group of movie devotees. Its existence became all the more important when the town's small cinema closed down shortly afterwards—meaning a lengthy trip to Perth for anyone who wanted to see the latest releases. Frustrated by the lack of variety on offer, the members hired more obscure movies, particularly those with French subtitles, for regular film nights in local hotels.

Jim was one of a long line of McGregors who had made Crieff their home—his great great grandfather, James, worked as a stonemason during the construction of the school in 1860. Jim's father, also James, seems to have had a more colourful history. The son of yet another James, who fought with the Black Watch in the First World War, he worked as a stonemason and fitter, and at the Hydro hotel. In 1936 he married his sweetheart Isabella Macindoe in Gretna Green, the little village on the border between Scotland and England that has long been a sanctuary for couples wanting to get married, without necessarily wanting others to know about it. Isabella was the daughter of a former consul to the Chilean government, and their marriage certificate records a simple ceremony in which Sarah Armstrong, of Gretna, and Mary

Little, of Carlisle, acted as witnesses to the wedding of a 21-year-old bachelor and his 20-year-old girlfriend who lived just a few streets from each other almost 200 miles away.

If Ewan McGregor's acting talent is in any way hereditary, it seems likely that it originated on his mother's side of the family. While Carol spent a dedicated and fulfilling career in teaching, her younger brother Denis pursued an acting dream that would later prove an inspiration to her son.

Carol and Denis Lawson were both born in Glasgow, the children of a jeweller and watchmaker, Laurie, and a confectionery saleswoman, then housewife, then jeweller, Phyllis. In 1953, when Carol was nine and Denis six, the family moved to Crieff, perhaps because Phyllis' own family were originally from that area, to open a jeweller's shop in the town. They quickly became popular within a community so small that everyone knew everyone else. For nearly 30 years Laurie and Phyllis built a solid reputation for their jewellery business, moving to new premises on the High Street shortly before Laurie's death. He had specialised in repairing watches and clocks, and is remembered by many as a gentle, likeable man who knew the names of all his customers. Phyllis recovered from the loss to continue running the business which still operates successfully today.

Friends recall the couple's frequent appearances at dance halls, fondly remembering how, although they may have been getting on a bit, they could still show the youngsters a thing or two. "Mrs Lawson was always elegant in the dancing," said Reverend Sandy Tait, a former minister at

Crieff South Church. "Performing the tango, she is a sight to behold."

Both children went to school at Morrison's, after which Carol went into teaching, while Denis, aged just 15, left Crieff in 1962 to become a carpet salesman in Dundee. As he later recalled: "I was the world's worst carpet salesman and the place closed down shortly after I left."

His heart was set, however, on a career in acting, and this finally led to a place in drama school back in Glasgow. From there he went on to perform in repertory theatre for a number of years, before moving to London in the early 1970s, the city he still calls home.

The Crieff that Ewan McGregor grew up in was a rural, middle-class town that had gradually acquired an image as a tranquil resting place for people heading into old age. It tended only to get clogged up by traffic when too many bus loads of pensioners had decided to go there for tea on the same day. The town's most significant landmark was a hotel, the Crieff Hydro, while its High Street was cluttered with an array of shops selling tartan rugs, tweed jumpers and numerous souvenirs to keep the seemingly endless procession of elderly visitors happy. The attitude of the 6,000 or so residents was illustrated by the fact that Crieff was one of the last remaining areas in Scotland to vote Conservative. Only in recent years have the Scottish Nationalists begun to seize the political initiative.

Situated in the rural calm of the Perthshire hills, Crieff in the 1970s was insulated from many of the vices of modern society. It was a place where people still dressed in tweeds and flat caps and drove Morris Minors—this at a time when bell-bottoms and Kevin Keegan perms were all the rage. As local councillor Ian Hunter put it: "People tended to give the impression that [Crieff] was stuck in some sort of time-warp."

In many ways, Crieff represented a world that had, for the most part, vanished. For the inhabitants it was a place where the spirit of those gentler times lingered on.

Just 50 miles further south the story could not have been more different. In Glasgow, gangland feuds and grinding poverty cast a long dark shadow over the city's reputation. In the run-down, derelict centre of the "No Mean City", people lived with the fear of becoming victims of violent crime. Across in Edinburgh, the architecturally stunning and culturally conservative capital was being engulfed by a wave of drug abuse, on a scale that Scotland had never seen before. As heroin addicts overdosed in record numbers, and shared needles spread the infection of the dreaded HIV, Edinburgh would become known as the AIDS capital of Europe.

Crieff was only an hour's drive away from the problems of the inner cities, but the locals' only real knowledge of drugs and violence came from the newspapers, or grave discussions involving much tutting and nodding of heads in the town's cosy tearooms. Crieff was small, safe, and virtually free from crime.

It was in these somewhat old-fashioned surroundings that Ewan McGregor spent his childhood. As a restless adolescent he would find the town's limitations too restrictive, but for a carefree youngster its open spaces provided a wonderful playground.

After Ewan was born, Jim and Carol had their hands full coping with the joys and traumas of bringing up a young family. Although both parents were newly qualified teachers, their pay was still relatively poor, and their home, "Edgemont", named after the road they had lived in in Glasgow, was a drab concrete semi-detached bungalow on Sauchie Terrace, in a less affluent area of the town.

The environment in which Ewan grew up was loving, stable and supportive, and his parents' priority in life was to ensure the right start for Ewan and his brother Colin. As a child, Ewan was a wide-eyed lad, eager to explore and learn, rarely seen without a smile on his face, or an excited glint in his eyes. On one occasion, however, an angry outburst led him to run away from home. For an hour he sat on The Knock, a large hill that overlooks Crieff, before returning home for tea with his tail between his legs. "He left because he was fed up with everybody," remembered Carol, who was so unperturbed by his actions that she made a packed lunch for him and told him to take their pet dog. "I knew he would go up The Knock and a friend of ours actually met him when he was up there with the dog, sitting under a tree, looking fed up."

His earliest memory, he said in an interview with *The Face*, was of dropping a Fry's Chocolate Cream bar into the River Earn when he was just two, and crying uncontrollably about the loss for a long time afterwards. Hardly a great trauma, in what was an otherwise remarkably happy and trouble-free beginning to his life.

Ewan's best pal was Jimmy Kerr, who lived two doors down in Sauchie Terrace. They would constantly run about together, fascinated by plastic go-karts that were popular at the time. When they were not playing with the go-karts, cardboard boxes provided hours of amusement. Indeed, their parents never ceased to be amazed by just how much entertainment children could get from a simple cardboard box. Like all best pals at that age, Ewan and Jimmy spent the rest of their time knocking lumps out of each other.

Although the bungalow had been a decent enough home, with two growing boys Jim and Carol needed somewhere bigger. As one neighbour recalled, there were also problems with damp. She remembered one occasion when Jim McGregor stormed into their house raging. "A lot of the houses in this street suffered from damp at that time," she said. "Jim wasn't too happy when he came in to see us after talking to the builders. They had given him a ridiculous answer to his problem. They told him he shouldn't have allowed kids to live in his house in the first place. Naturally he was extremely angry."

Not long afterwards the McGregors moved house. With Jim's new position of housemaster at Morrison's came the benefit of living in a much nicer house on the more affluent side of the High Street. Their new home, "The Hermitage", was a plush, three-bedroom Victorian house set in a tree-lined lane. Young Ewan even had his own room, looking out on to a large back garden. For Jim McGregor the new house was ideal, as it was only a short walk from the grounds of Morrison's Academy. He had been educated there, and now his two sons were about to follow in his footsteps.

II

SCHOOL'S OUT

Ewan McGregor entered the primary section of Morrison's Academy at the age of five. His first taste of education had been at a private nursery in Crieff Hydro and then, in keeping with family tradition, he followed his parents and many other relatives into Morrison's.

In Crieff, Morrison's was more than just a school, it was an institution built on more than a hundred years of tradition. From the day its doors opened in 1860, it had established a reputation as a centre of educational excellence for the cream of society. At that time the pupils were the children of the upper classes, wealthy businessmen and service families.

The school Ewan attended had made some concessions to

the modern world—nowadays it accepted girls—but it still retained its reputation for high standards and strict discipline. Inside Morrison's hallowed halls, pupils were only allowed to walk on the left-hand side of the corridors, risking drastic consequences if they dared cross the line. Running was also forbidden, and silence rigorously enforced.

Morrison's was a school for both day and boarding pupils. Ewan arrived in the morning and went home in the evening, but those in the boarding school were sometimes only allowed outside the grounds at weekends. When they did venture into town, school uniform had to be worn. Indeed, few standards were enforced as strictly as the dress code, according to Iain King, one of Ewan's friends at the school. He remembered how Morrison's pupils stood out in their brightly-coloured outfits. The tie had navy blue, maroon and white stripes, and shirts had to be white or grey. The compulsory navy blue blazer was never complete without a maroon and white braid around every edge. When the weather was colder— which in Crieff meant most of the year—pupils were also encouraged to wear grey V-neck sweaters.

Iain King hated the uniform, and it seems most of the 600 other pupils at Morrison's felt the same way. "It's fair to say we stood out in Crieff when we were walking down the street," he recalled. "The short navy trousers went down to our knees, and we wore red socks with them until third year. Then presumably they considered us old enough to wear long trousers with grey socks. If you were caught with red socks on under the long trousers you got it for that."

Ewan's seven years in the primary section were both happy and conventional, and although he showed few signs of academic excellence, he got on well with the other pupils. Despite tending to lack concentration in classes, his performance was adequate.

Like most boys of his age, Ewan could be quiet and well-behaved, even charming when he wanted to be, but if ever a bit of fun was brewing, he was quick to join in. On one occasion, when Ewan was 11, Iain King remembered a Primary Seven class in uproar as an exasperated teacher tried in vain to control the situation. Suddenly there was complete silence, as every pupil froze and stared ahead, open mouthed.

King explained: "We were being taught Latin but for some reason, which I can't remember, the class had become completely out of control. Everyone was at it, and the more the teacher tried to tell us to be quiet, the more we refused to settle down. Then she got so worked up that her false teeth came flying out of her mouth and landed on the floor between a couple of the desks. No-one could quite believe what had happened. For a few seconds everyone shut up. Then it started again."

By the time he entered the secondary school at Morrison's later that year, Ewan's confidence was growing. Popular with those who knew him, he was developing an ability to charm that became one of the most striking aspects of his personality. In those tasks that required creativity, he shone. He became an accomplished musician, playing drums in the school pipe band and with a local ceilidh band. He won a prize for mastering the French horn, which he went on to play in a performance, with fellow-pupil James Mason, of "an arrangement of the 18th-century sea-song 'Tom Bowling' by Mr Andrews, who accompanied them on a somewhat erratic organ." Ewan also learned to play the guitar, and was the drummer in a short-lived rock group, Scarlet Pride, which split up when he left school.

An accomplished singer, Ewan performed impressively in the school choir, and won a prize for a vocal duet with his brother Colin. The McGregor brothers received a glowing review in the school magazine, *The Morrisonian*, for another joint effort—a humorous rendition of "Brush Up Your Shakespeare". Their participation in the choir party also rated a mention, when they satirised various members of the choir—including themselves.

In sport, however, Ewan tried hard but rarely excelled. Classmates said Jim McGregor gave his son a harder time than others during PE classes to avoid the inevitable allegations of favouritism, although his treatment of his son was never unfair.

Ewan was never keen to run about a muddy field for too long, and his sporting achievements were limited. He played in the second XV rugby team in the position of hooker, and was reckoned to be a possible wicket-keeper in the making for the cricket team, but that was as far as he progressed. Instead, his talents lay in an instinctive feel for all things creative. His sharp wit and eloquence showed he was bright, while his musical skills and early acting exploits proved he had the ability to do well in areas that appealed to him.

But, as is so often the case, he found it increasingly difficult to respond to the demands made upon him at Morrison's. Schools typically regarded artistic subjects as little more than a sideline, offering limited prospects of a worthwhile career. Instead, it was pupils' achievements in traditional subjects like English, Maths and Science that were used in assessing their progress. McGregor was considered an average student—hardly a complete failure, but still falling short of what the teachers expected.

At 15 he entered fourth year, and began to experience the stresses of approaching national exams, the dreaded O-Grades. Passing these would lead to Highers the following year, which in turn provided a ticket to university. The pressures upon him were undoubtedly intensified by comparisons with his older brother Colin—who was academically brilliant, a sporting hero, and head boy to boot.

"Ewan couldn't compete with his brother in sport," said Jim McGregor. "Colin was very good athletically, particularly at rugby, but Ewan couldn't match him and I think he always felt they were being compared."

As his classmate Fergus Adams recalled, the omens for Ewan were not good. "He was a great guy, and always a good laugh," said Adams. "But he was never going to match up to his older brother who was superb academically and even better at sport."

As the pressure increased, Ewan's normally happy,

contented persona was replaced by a restless, confused mind at odds with the demands being placed upon him. It was common knowledge that he wanted to be an actor, but no-one seemed to be taking him seriously. Jane Kennedy, a schoolfriend who remembered being worried by his moodiness, told how he suddenly began to drift away from his friends. "Ewan was confident, happy and joined in with anything that was going on," she said. "We were close-knit. There was even a strong bond between the boarders and the day pupils, and he was part of that big family. He could also, sometimes, be quite quiet, but not often.

"I remember when he was about 16 he withdrew very much from the crowd. It was noticeable he wasn't as happy. He became much quieter, and didn't get so involved with people. I remember in the playground he never used to join in with the usual banter. He wouldn't be as bad as standing on his own, but he would stick to his closest friends. There was obviously a lot on his mind."

Like many youngsters, Ewan had been keen on watching films on television. The difference was that his interest went deeper—he would spend Saturdays watching ancient black and white movies, rather than the sports programmes to which any other young boy would have been glued. He loved the glamorous atmosphere created by Ealing or Hollywood, and would sometimes watch four films in one day. Like his Uncle Denis, Ewan dreamed of one day being part of this exciting fantasy world. Stuck in school, frustrated and disillusioned, little did he realise that his adult life was destined to become a realisation of these childhood dreams.

According to *The Scotsman*, McGregor said of his time at Morrison's: "I didn't hate school. I just didn't get it." Although popular there, he still felt a deep sense of insecurity, and in an interview with *Neon* magazine he spoke of an "incredible desire to be loved and wanted, which is also a lot to do with acting: 'Please like me. Oh fucking please, everybody like me.' "

He also harboured a growing dislike for the teachers who failed to understand the reasons for his lack of commitment to his studies, and his increasingly rebellious ways. He has often told how he became depressed, but never noticed it himself, and admits he "went off the rails" for a while. "I didn't realise it at the time, but apparently I was," he said.

The root of some of his problems lay in his desire to study both art and music. When it came to choosing his courses at the age of 15, Ewan was told he had to drop either art or music in favour of a more traditional subject.

"I had a great love for music and art, but they don't really let you do that," he said. "They think you are copping out, which was a shame. That basically knocked it on the head for me. I became less interested."

McGregor later recalled how he had problems with a particular teacher, although he declined to reveal her identity. "She was a Jean Brodie type," he said. "We'd been quite close, but then she started pushing me in a particular direction. Anyway, I started answering back and she kept sending me to the headmaster." "[It] was perhaps starting to get embarrassing for my father."

After passing four O-Grades—an average result—Ewan pleaded with his parents to allow him to leave school to pursue his acting dreams. "I felt I had something to live up to a bit," he said, referring to his brother who went on to become a fighter pilot in the RAF. "But there was no pressure from anyone. I was just losing interest, desperate to start, to get away. There was never any question of me doing anything else, never, ever. But I never imagined I'd be allowed to leave."

At first he wasn't. The school's rector Harry Ashmall and other teachers tried to impress on him the importance of qualifications when he returned after a miserable summer break for a reluctant start to fifth year, and the daunting prospect of Higher exams. But it soon became clear that his academic career was coming to an end. Maths went so poorly it was decided he should do a typing course instead. Finally, his parents backed down, realising that their son was digging himself into an ever deeper hole. They resigned themselves to being there for him if his venture into the big, bad world ended in tears.

Carol believed the best way forward for Ewan was to leave school. "I think there was a period when he was unhappy because he was being pressured by me and by other people into more concentrated study than he preferred to give it," she said. "And I think it was quite a surprise to him that we did that, because he was just in his fifth year and that was the year of his Highers. I felt he would be far happier and get on better if he just left and got a job."

At around the same time, the McGregors moved home again, this time to a large bungalow beside a glen about ten miles east of Crieff. With rain battering against the windows as they returned home in the car one stormy night, Carol turned to her restless son who was moping in the back seat.

"Son, we've thought about it, and if you want to leave, that's fine by us. If you're unhappy it's not necessarily going to do you much good to stay on."

Ewan later said: "She was right, and it was a really brave decision for them to make." "They didn't make me feel bad about it. They were cool about this crisis and that was a huge relief."

The decision was taken with one proviso: Ewan was to find a place in college.

Years later, in February 1997, he returned to Morrison's to give a one-off acting master-class. When the media had left, he also paid a visit to the state-run Crieff High School, where his mother had taught.

Asked by pupils at Morrison's if he regretted "bailing out" early, McGregor told them: "I don't regret it at all, no. What I do regret, however, is not having realised that what you are taught in school is maybe valid. I never really made the connection that what you were being taught was useful in any way. I never thought it was and I was wrong in that respect."

By the time he returned to his old school, Ewan McGregor

had fulfilled many of his dreams, but the young man who had left Morrison's nine years earlier could hardly have dared hope that things would turn out as they had done. Jim and Carol McGregor had allowed their son the freedom to realise his destiny. It soon became apparent that their faith in him was fully justified.

III

AN ACTOR'S LIFE FOR ME

Ewan McGregor's decision to abandon his education in favour of a life less ordinary was a controversial one. In a place like Crieff, most people could not believe this teenager was turning his back on the well-worn path of school and university for a future that was at best uncertain. Few said anything to his face, saving their opinions until his back was turned, but they thought he was crazy. According to friends, one of his closest pals, Malcolm Copland, even told him so, sparking a bust-up between the pair.

But for Ewan McGregor there was no turning back. He loved his friends and the strong community spirit of the people of his home town—but for them, exams paved the way to a safe, traditional lifestyle, usually in Crieff. For Ewan one of the attractions of acting was that it offered the exact opposite—challenge, uncertainty and risk.

Crieff was too "tweedy". "You get out of there at sixteen if you want to do other things," he once said.

His final year in school had been fraught with difficulties, and his mood had become unusually sullen, with frequent bouts of depression and unruliness worrying close friends and his parents. But despite all this, he had remained focused on the pursuit of his ultimate goal. As Jim McGregor said later: "From the moment he could walk he always wanted to be an actor." By the time he was 14, Ewan was hounding the repertory theatre in Perth for work. Finally, a couple of weeks after leaving school, he got his chance, as an extra in a production of *A Passage to India*, in which he was blacked up before "running around the stage with a turban on".

According to Ewan McGregor, his decision to become an actor was made when he was only nine. But his interest in acting could be traced back to a much younger age. When he went to see his uncle in a pantomime at the tender age of two, his parents remember him being entranced by the colour and movement on stage.

At the age of five, Ewan made his stage debut as the Sheriff of Nottingham in a school production of *Robin Hood*. Few people witnessed the classroom performance organised by his teacher, Helen McGregor (no relation), but, as the villain of the piece, the young McGregor was apparently as convincing as a five-year-old could be.

Two girls in the Primary One class, Yvonne McIldowie and Caroline Hoskins, were given slightly less demanding roles as trees. One thing they recall clearly about the performance is that Ewan remembered all his lines, a remarkable feat for a youngster who was not yet able to read. Undoubtedly, the aspiring actor would have been helped by his parents, who were once again to hand when another starring role cropped up the following year in a play at the church where he attended Sunday School.

On a cold Sunday evening the week before Christmas in 1977, two hundred proud parents watched their children tackle the biblical epic, *David and Goliath*. The play—using dialogue taken directly from the holy book itself—attempted to illustrate the theme of good always triumphing over evil. Unfortunately, most of the one hundred children involved could not read the Bible, let alone understand it, and so it was hardly surprising that the final result was something of a shambles. In any case, a shadow hung over the proceedings, as the local theatre-loving laird, Sir William Murray, who had donated the lighting for the production, had taken his own life shortly before the performance.

The production was directed by the minister at Crieff South Church, Reverend Sandy Tait, who put most of its failings down to not heeding the traditional theatrical warning about never working with children. "My experience of children and acting was always that they required an awful lot of cajoling, prodding, pushing and threatening before they would do anything half right," he said, candidly.

Reverend Tait had only one difficulty with young Ewan. "We got a call from the minister to say there was a problem and could we come and see him," said Jim McGregor. "We wondered what Ewan could have done. But we discovered that the minister had found out he couldn't read."

"There were a lot of lines and the minister was in a bit of a panic," recalled Carol. "So I said that by the time it came to doing it, Ewan would know the lines, and I just read them to him every night and we practised it at home until we knew it virtually word perfect."

Ewan McGregor's role was quite complicated, but the six-year-old triumphed as though acting was second nature. Even at this early stage, his determination to get things exactly right did not go unnoticed. Reverend Tait, who had also been an impressive actor as a child, said Ewan reminded him of the potential he himself had shown at an early age. On one occasion shortly before the only rehearsal, he found the youngster alone in the church practising his lines. "I can't remember how Ewan came to be in the Sunday School nor can I remember how he got the part in the play," he said. "But when I saw the production I recognised in Ewan what I had seen in myself. This child had a natural flair. And that was rare."

In the privacy of his own diary, the minister wrote what was to be Ewan's first review. "The play went well enough but it really is a ragged affair. Wee Ewan McGregor was outstandingly good, however, as David."

Years later Reverend Tait would receive an unexpected

telephone call from Carol McGregor. "She said Ewan had just got his first big break and told me I was the first to know because I had given him his first part," he said. "I thought that was so very touching, and very kind."

At the same time in 1977 that Ewan McGregor made his first stage appearance, the world was getting to grips with the movie phenomenon known as *Star Wars*. Whether it was because of the ground-breaking special effects, the inter-galactic storyline, or the swashbuckling characters, the film was enjoying massive international success.

In Crieff, the anticipation was even greater because local celebrity Denis Lawson had a small part in the film. No doubt Ewan McGregor could hardly contain himself at the thought of seeing his Uncle Denis in the role of X-wing fighter pilot Wedge Antilles. Spotting him on the screen, however, was not easy. Not only was Lawson in the film for only a few minutes, but every time he appeared on screen he was hidden behind a large helmet, and seemed to have developed a strange American accent.

Even so, for the young McGregor it was a hugely exciting time. He had always admired his Uncle Denis, who was often on television, and who, when he came home to Crieff, usually arrived in a sleek Cadillac. He sported long hair, big side-burns, and hippy clothes—including brightly coloured beads, a sheepskin waistcoat and massive flares. Most impressive of all, Uncle Denis wore no shoes. All this was in marked contrast to the tweedy, conservative inhabitants of his home town.

"He gave people flowers," said McGregor. "He was an extraordinary character and I would go: 'Who is this man?' I wanted to be different like him."

"We would always go out as a family when Denis came home," recalled Jim McGregor, "and he and Ewan clicked. They were a real duo, always clowning around."

Perth's little Odeon cinema had never seen anything quite like it when the *Star Wars* bandwagon finally rolled into town in 1978. The cinema was sold out for weeks as the locals enjoyed a couple of hours of pure escapism.

The day Ewan was taken to see the movie, school seemed to last forever. When the bell finally rang, he charged across the playground and waited impatiently for his mother to turn up. She drove him the 15 miles to Perth, where they joined the long queue outside the cinema. When they finally took their seats, they were not disappointed—Ewan got to see his Uncle Denis on the big screen for the first time. Even so, it was Carrie Fisher who made the biggest impression of all. "He fell in love with Princess Leia," said a friend. "He reckons that was his first crush."

Soon afterwards Ewan joined a procession through the streets of Crieff to celebrate his uncle's involvement in the film. That day, remembers local historian Colin Mayell, the town witnessed scenes the like of which it will never see again. "I walked in front of a procession dressed up as the arch villain Darth Vader," said Mayell, who had recently returned to the town after fleeing from the revolution in Iran. "Denis Lawson was the big celebrity and he was walking behind me. Well, I had this bloody great mask on, waving the light-sabre, and the children seemed to love it. I'm sure they were impressed. Afterwards in the car park I was in the back of the car changing, and my trousers were off. The next thing I heard was a small boy's voice shouting: 'There's Darth Vader changing his breeks.' I had to sneak away quietly after that."

Long after *Star Wars* had departed from Perth, McGregor and the other local children were still captivated by its appeal. Even McGregor's bed was adorned with *Star Wars* sheets and pillow-cases. But no-one had been more impressed by the film than his pal, Alastair Maclachlan, who assembled the equivalent of a *Star Wars* shrine in his parents' attic. Maclachlan became a *Star Wars* version of a Trekkie—if he didn't have a certain kind of plastic figure, it probably didn't exist.

Ewan McGregor and his big brother Colin spent many contented hours at Maclachlan's house in Drummond Terrace playing with these toys. According to Maclachlan, so did most of the young male population of Crieff. "My attic was full of the figures and Ewan would come round often to play with them," he said, recalling the extraordinary fight scenes that took place below his attic skylight. "Everyone knew Ewan's uncle had been in the film, but Ewan didn't really have any of the toys himself. It is quite amazing to think that the boy who used to come round to my house to play with all that stuff is to be a face on the new figures."

Undoubtedly, films like *Star Wars* were a major factor in Ewan's decision that the actor's life was for him, but he regularly cites two other reasons: the inspiration of his uncle, naturally enough, and his love of pantomimes, even as a very young boy—particularly because the role of the leading man was always played by a woman, who wore stockings. And there lay the core of the fascination.

"It all became about legs and I fell in love with the leading ladies," he said. "So, it had a lot to do with sex."

Ewan's spare time, when he wasn't acting in the latest class play, or lying on the sofa immersed in old movies, was spent with his gang of friends. On The Knock, Ewan and his pals would keep themselves amused for hours re-enacting scenes from films like *Grease*. "One of us would be Olivia, and another would be John," he said. "I was a very good Olivia Newton John. I don't think there was any touching or kissing involved, you know. We were just kids."

As the boys grew older, so more traditional pursuits were acted out on The Knock. Ewan and close pal Eric Strickland built a den of fern and twigs of which he said "the SAS would be proud". The two boys would often hide there for hours, using their catapults to fire fir-cones at passing pony trekkers and young girls. Oblivious to the potential consequences, the rear end of a horse was often the target—a direct hit resulting in the horse taking off, with its rider hanging on for dear life. The boys also amused themselves by launching fireworks at innocent bystanders. "We got up to a lot of mischief," recalled close friend Malcolm Copland.

"We'd lay [fireworks] on the road, light them, and they would shoot along at a group of people ahead. I suppose fir-cones were a far safer option."

When Ewan wasn't with his pals annoying ramblers on The Knock, he mucked out stables at Crieff Hydro and learned to ride. He also enjoyed sub-aqua diving and swimming. Along with Copland, he spent his teenage holidays waiting on tables at the nearby Murraypark Hotel.

It was around this time that Ewan McGregor almost made a premature exit from the stage of life. Fed up during a school holiday when all his mates were away, he went out on his bike and ended up racing down a steep hill at full speed straight into a busy street. As he lost control and hit the road with an almighty thud, cars and lorries swerved to avoid him. It was the kind of lucky escape that might have featured in the films of Harold Lloyd or Buster Keaton, but it still resulted in a short stay in hospital for the teenager while he got over the effects of concussion.

This nasty blow to the head inflicted only temporary damage and certainly did not affect his desire to make it as an actor. Yvonne McIldowie, who sat next to him in third year chemistry, remembers him saying that some day he would be James Bond. "It was intended as a bit of a joke, of course, but you could tell deep down that's what he really wanted," said McIldowie, who is delighted by McGregor's subsequent success, and believes that the day is not far away when the keys to 007's Aston Martin will be his. "He didn't make a big thing about wanting to be an actor at school but everyone knew that's what he was going to do. And I think few people round here will be surprised by the success he has had. He was always extremely determined and knew exactly where he was going. He got a job washing cars after leaving school and some people commented on what a waster he was. Now I hope those same people are big enough to admit how wrong they were."

In 1985, around the same time he was rehearsing "The name's Bond—James Bond" to his classmate, Morrison's celebrated its 125th anniversary. The Queen came to Crieff for the occasion, and the school faithfully upheld the tradition of having Her Majesty believe the world smells of wet paint— by ordering some last-minute brushwork just feet from where she was standing.

"We did a revue to mark the 125th anniversary and it was lots of fun," said Alastair Maclachlan. "Ewan came up on stage and did this long poem on his own. Everyone else was having a bit of a laugh but he was taking it very seriously. When he came on stage you instantly knew that he knew exactly what he was doing. He was very professional, very confident, very good."

On another occasion Ewan took a leading role in a school production of a French farce. As final preparations were under way, one teacher could not have known how true his prediction would turn out when he talked of imminent rave revues which would "take us to Hollywood."

The subsequent edition of *The Morrisonian* described the performance as the "most enjoyable play of the year", while

Ewan McGregor, "despite an excessive wig" was "a vigorous Leslie, the romantic lead."

All this was in marked contrast to Ewan McGregor's first appearance on TV, playing with the school band. During the show, which appeared on Grampian Television, the local ITV channel in the north of Scotland, Ewan wiped his nose on his sleeve in between playing passages from Mozart on the French horn. He did so because he thought it looked cool, unaware the cameras were trying to avoid him by cutting to close-ups of the pianist. Ewan came to regret the prank, as Jim McGregor would later entertain his son's girlfriends by showing them the embarrassing video of his TV debut.

Ewan's attitude to acting, however, was far more serious, and helped him win his opportunity at Perth Repertory Theatre. He had been writing and phoning constantly for two years, but without success. With a little help from his mother, who explained Ewan's plight to the theatre's director, Joan Knight, the 16-year-old was eventually offered the chance to get his foot on the first rung of the acting ladder as a £50-a-week stagehand. He seized the opportunity with both hands, and was soon putting up and pulling down stage sets with the rest of the crew, as well as developing his acting skills in the recently established youth theatre. Ewan McGregor had made the first step on the long road that would lead to international stardom.

IV

THE CAPED CRUSADER
OF KIRKCALDY

The town of Perth is known historically as the gateway to the Highlands, and it was here that Ewan McGregor took his first tentative steps into the world of the theatre. The repertory theatre that provided this ambitious teenager with his first taste of the business had a fine reputation—well-known British actors like Gordon Jackson and Edward Woodward had cut their teeth there, and Joan Knight, the director at the time of McGregor's arrival, was regarded as a formidable figure in Scottish theatre.

Knight was keen to give a chance to local youngsters with

talent and a willingness to work hard, and so when Carol McGregor explained her son's situation, and assured Knight he had the sort of ability she was looking for, the director extended a warm hand of welcome.

Initially, Ewan worked as a member of the scene-shifting crew while developing his raw acting talents in youth theatre workshops. He soon discovered there was a great deal to learn—and not only in the theatre, as he came across real-life situations he had never encountered back home in the more sheltered surroundings of Crieff.

"You know, 'Someone's having an affair and he's married with kids,' and I'd never seen that before," he recalled. "Or 'He's gay'. I'd never seen that before. All these different things are just part of life that I didn't know anything about." He recalled being mortified during a conversation amongst the crew about apartheid—he didn't know what it was.

At first, McGregor stood out not because of his ability, but his incessant querying and questioning of actors, directors and stage crew. He was keen to know everything, and in hindsight felt his persistence may have left his older colleagues somewhat exasperated. "Suddenly I was where I wanted to be and my life went into wide-screen," he said. "I had a ball and the depression lifted. But I was also a real pain in the backside because I was so keen. The people there remember me as a nightmare. I wanted to do everything—this, this, this and this—and they would tell me to shut up." He reckoned his fellow crew thought he was an "arsehole".

They, however, remember him differently. He seemed a

good deal more mature than his seventeen years, and his charming manner ensured that he never rubbed people up the wrong way. "Ewan was a good laugh," said Ian Grieve, a member of the crew who worked alongside McGregor. "He certainly wasn't an arse."

The backstage boys at Perth were a motley crew of academics, bikers, and students, all of whom were would-be actors. As one of the youngest in the group, the potential was there for McGregor to be given a hard time by some of his more experienced colleagues. But he more than held his own. "He was quiet and tended to keep himself to himself, but he wasn't antisocial," added Grieve, who said McGregor coped admirably during the regular banter. "The crew were mostly biker types who looked like they hadn't washed for a week. But they were really erudite—there was always a copy of *Zen and the Art of Motorcycle Maintenance* lying around. It was that kind of place. Usually the topic of conversation would get round to the guy who couldn't do the job properly and they would take a fair deal of stick, but that was never Ewan. He was good at the job, and willing to learn what he didn't know. He enjoyed himself while he was working, and the other lads enjoyed his company. The impression you got was that he knew exactly what he was about, what he wanted to do with his life, and that he would do it. We knew his uncle was Denis Lawson but he never made any play of that. He was very down-to-earth."

The job was poorly paid, and involved hard, physical work, but the benefits far outweighed the disadvantages for those who wanted to learn the trade. During the panto season, the crew virtually lived in the theatre for a month of twice-daily performances. Most productions required the dreaded overnight shift—to take down the scenery after the final performance. Grieve remembered McGregor toiling until the sun came up after the last night of *Pravda*. But the most boring and mundane job was that of the spot operator, directing the spotlight on to a cast member on stage. Other members of the crew noticed that McGregor tackled even this most tedious of jobs with his customary boundless enthusiasm.

The youth theatre director, Liz Carruthers, observed him during the regular workshops. "We did lots of workshops that year, but to be honest, I don't remember Ewan being particularly outstanding in any way," said Liz. "I think he learned a hell of a lot during that period. We would always see him chatting to actors and crew, and talking to directors as well. Every little bit of information was important to him. But I don't believe any of us would have possibly imagined him playing Obi-Wan Kenobi in *Star Wars* just a few years down the line."

The real significance of all his hard work at Perth was that it provided McGregor with the experience he needed to win a place on one of only two foundation drama courses in Scotland. With only twenty-six places up for grabs at his preferred choice, Kirkcaldy College of Technology, he faced stiff opposition from around two hundred other applicants.

His performance at interview in Kirkcaldy convinced staff

that he had what it took to make the grade on the one-year course. First, he read a dramatic piece and performed some dance exercises, then he was encouraged to take part in drama games. The questioning was intense, but the lecturers were impressed by his willingness to come out of his shell in an alien environment, a key quality they always looked for.

In August 1988, at the age of seventeen, McGregor finally left home. Like any other teenager, he was apprehensive about fending for himself for the first time, without the support of his family to fall back on. But at long last he was on the way to realising his acting dream.

"I loved Crieff," he said. "But it's the kind of place I eventually wanted to leave. That's nothing against the place itself, but there isn't a great acting industry in Crieff, so obviously I had to get out."

On arrival in Kirkcaldy, McGregor was more than a little surprised when he opened the door of his room, number G14, only to be confronted by what seemed to be a large cupboard. Surely there must have been some mistake? There wasn't. In front of him was a tiny, sparsely decorated area, no more than ten feet by six feet, crammed into which were a single bed, a desk, a chair, a wardrobe, a wash hand basin and an easy chair. If he breathed in, there was just enough space for McGregor too. This was to be his home for the next nine months. Down the corridor was a room that contained a bath and no shower. McGregor was to share this with five other students—preferably not at the same time. The eighty or so students who squeezed into three floors of the college's halls of residence were also provided with a cramped common room where they could watch TV, or form a queue to play table-tennis.

The halls building itself was one of those concrete disasters that planners threw up in the 1960s. It was, they said, intended to look from above like Scotland's national emblem, the thistle—a novel concept only pilots were able to appreciate. Those who lived there tried to imagine what kind of person could conceive and erect such a monstrosity. It was an embarrassing blot on an already bleak landscape. "It's the worst building I've ever seen in my life," said a classmate of McGregor's. "You simply have to see it to believe it."

The halls were positioned in the centre of the town pronounced Kircoddy, a small place situated in southern Fife, on the banks of the River Forth. The halls housed a mixture of male and female students, but only boys were allocated rooms on the ground floor. This was no coincidence, according to halls' warden Tom Lawrence, but rather a deliberate ploy to maximise security—the male shield would provide a first line of defence against any perverts who attempted to make an unannounced visit.

Kirkcaldy College was a technical college intended mainly for local lads who wanted to learn skills such as building, joinery, carpentry and other manual trades. It was an unlikely home for a drama course that attracted students of a more artistic nature from all over the country. And when they got there, the would-be actors generally did their best to keep as far away as possible from the would-be woodworkers.

Because they were based at different sites, this was usually no problem. But once a week the luvvies were required to venture into enemy territory for a stage carpentry class with lecturer Ally Kippen. It was often a disturbing experience.

"Some of the drama students were pretty worried when they had to go across to the Nairn Campus for that class," recalled one staff member. "They were a completely different breed from the guys who were training to be builders. They had, shall we say, separate outlooks on life. It was an uneasy co-existence. The boys over at Nairn thought acting was a bit sissy and didn't hold back in being forward about it. The drama kids got a bit of stick, and they were usually delighted when they got back in one piece. Some would go down the pub for a few drinks to calm the nerves."

For this reason, the students on the foundation arts course—real title Higher National Certificate Theatre Arts Programme—tended to keep to themselves. But they had virtually no choice anyway. The long hours they worked, sometimes up to twelve a day, allowed them little time to get to know students on other courses, even if they wanted to.

The drama course itself consisted of a series of modules, officially lasting twenty-three hours each week. But in reality the heavy workload kept them on campus much longer. The hands-on nature of the course meant every class had to put together four complete productions a year, and as a result students often toiled away late into the night to meet deadlines. But hard work did not worry McGregor, and the co-director of drama, Lynn Bains, was particularly impressed by his keenness and willingness to learn every aspect of his craft. "From the minute he walked in the door he was enthusiastic, willing to do anything you threw at him. He was talented and very hard-working," she said.

McGregor and the other students were put through an intense nine months intended to provide a grounding in all areas of theatre; from acting, voice, movement and dance to learning how to build stage scenery, and handle front-of-house work, publicity and promotion. By providing this basic knowledge, the course had gained a reputation as a stepping-stone for those who wanted to go on to more specialised and prestigious drama schools.

Drawing on the experience he had gained in Perth, McGregor worked as a stage manager on a revue shortly after the start of term. Overseeing the technical side of the production, he was responsible for everything from making sure the costumes fitted to ensuring any given piece of scenery was in the right place at the right time.

In the second term production, a performance of *The Prime of Miss Jean Brodie*, McGregor played the demanding part of the conservative music teacher who wants to marry Miss Brodie. The third term production, *A Few From The Fridge*, was a parody of Arthur Miller's celebrated work, *A View From The Bridge*. On this occasion McGregor combined a stage management role with a major part in the comedy. The play was well-received when it was taken out on the road for theatre workshop performances in Glasgow and Edinburgh. The final production of the year was a play called *Missfoot*, in which McGregor took a minor part while again focusing more on the stage management side. "It was a hard year," he said. "I had to do everything—make the sets, design costumes, publicise the play, act in it, stage manage it. For a young boy it was a lot of responsibility but I learned an awful lot and it was a great stepping-stone."

It became increasingly obvious as the course progressed that Ewan McGregor was destined for greater things, according to one of his closest friends at college, Paul Kininmonth. "We were all thrown in at the deep end which was great. Everyone wanted to get into acting but this gave us an overview of everything else that drama involves. It was hard work, but few people had a problem about that. When we started Ewan was interested in stage management, and he took a great interest in that throughout the course. By the end of the second show it was obvious there was more commitment and maturity being shown by the people in the class. It was also noticeable at that time just how much Ewan had grown in confidence with what he was doing. At the same time, there was no bullshit about him. If anyone was going to do well on the course, I reckoned at the time it would be him. He was so confident. He shone in everything he did."

These optimistic views were not shared by some of his lecturers. Maggie McMillan, who taught voice techniques, believed Ewan McGregor was only average, and nowhere near as talented as his classmate Jane Innes, who later starred in the TV detective series *Taggart*.

McMillan barely remembered his final-term speech test, in which he recited a soliloquy from Shakespeare's *Twelfth Night* and extracts from the work of Lenny Bruce. On the other hand, she vividly recalled Jane Innes' "magnificent" rendition of a Victoria Wood sketch. "Ewan's speeches passed, but they were far from wonderful," she said. "I'd love to say he was, but I never felt he was that outstanding when he was here. I had forgotten all about him, then he suddenly popped up on the TV."

In another end-of-year test, McGregor and classmate Andy Milarvie departed from the usual serious, sometimes intimate, dance routines, and opted for camp slapstick instead. With Ewan dressed as Batman, and Andy playing The Joker, the pair had their class in stitches with a hilarious routine. "I knew what they were planning so I deliberately put it at the end because it was a lovely way to finish," said college lecturer Rhonda Stephen. "It worked well . . . and they kept a few surprises from me. I hadn't seen the costumes until they appeared on stage."

In front of a backdrop resplendent with posters screaming "Zapp", "Kerpow" and "Biff", McGregor made his grand entrance, as the familiar Batman theme tune blared through the speakers. His home-made outfit consisted of a Bat mask, a dark blue cape, black T-shirt with the caped crusader's logo emblazoned on the front, and a thin yellow belt. Dark grey jogging trousers were tucked into blue football socks, and the outfit was rounded off with an ill-fitting pair of blue underpants over his trousers. When he improvised towards the end, using a kiddies' tricycle as the Batmobile, the class were close to hysterics. Not surprisingly, pass marks were awarded.

This was the crowning moment in a year which had reassured McGregor that his decision to go into acting was the right one.

"I realised this was exactly what I wanted to do, that I hadn't been mistaken all this time," he recalled later.

"He said that up until the year at Kirkcaldy he had felt people didn't have much faith that he would amount to much," said Lynn Bains, who had noticed a growing maturity in the teenager during his nine months at Kirkcaldy. "That period was a turning point in his life," said another staff member. "No-one could really have known he would have amounted to anything special, but we all liked him. He was very popular."

V

THE DRAMA PATIENTS

The little boy leant against the bus stop, clutching his Fruit Pastilles. It seemed like he had been waiting for ages. Just then, as he looked down the road one more time, he caught sight of the bus. At last. He was sure Mary Green would be on it. And he was sure she would like one of his sweets. She always did.

As the bus pulled slowly to a stop alongside the boy, a few people filtered down the steps. And there she was. Mary Green, her Morrison's Academy uniform almost identical to his own, bounded off the bus with her small leather satchel hanging over her shoulder.

Mary Green was Ewan McGregor's first girlfriend. They

were both nine and in the same class. Another classmate, Alastair Maclachlan, is convinced the couple sealed their friendship with a kiss—Mary Green, he believes, was Ewan McGregor's first kiss. "I'm sure he kissed Mary. They were always friends, and at that age it was entirely innocent," he said. The alleged lucky recipient remembers McGregor as her first "boyfriend", and she his first "girlfriend". But as for that kiss . . . "I honestly can't remember. At that time, he was my best pal and we were like two little kids being boyfriend and girlfriend. He would meet me off the bus from school with Fruit Pastilles, but I suppose I kind of two-timed him by becoming friendly with another boy called Donald who met me at the other end with Fruit Gums. I think it was the Fruit Gums that did it. I preferred them. Whether I kissed Ewan or not, I couldn't honestly tell you. We were very young, you know."

At that age, most boys react to girls by pulling their hair or calling them names. Ewan, on the other hand, seemed comfortable in their company, and had female friends. It was one of the many things he had in common with his Uncle Denis. More than 20 years earlier, friends remembered how Denis had got into trouble after being caught kissing girls at the bus stop outside the school.

From an early age, Ewan McGregor seemed to have a fascination with the opposite sex. He always fell in love with the leading lady in panto, and when *Grease* arrived on cinema screens, Ewan was smitten by Olivia Newton John. Just as young girls now cover their bedroom wall with images of

McGregor, as a sprightly six-year-old he suddenly found himself fascinated by the sexy pop singer turned actress who played Sandi.

At school, he was popular with the girls, but not because he was considered incredibly handsome—if anything his older brother had the edge over him on that too. At one point Colin even started dating a girl, Collette Besant, whom Ewan fancied. Instead, it was Ewan's personality and outgoing demeanour that were seen as his strong points. As with any other teenage boy, girlfriends came and went—including Susan Williams, Andrea Smith and Vicky McNally. Ewan McGregor's string of short flings never went too far, though. Sometimes he sneaked girls into the dark and empty cinema below the ballroom at the Crieff Hydro, where they would fondle innocently until rumbled by an annoyed porter.

His liaison with Vicky McNally provides a vivid example of a typical teenager finding out how to handle a relationship. Ewan was sixteen, and in the middle of his Billy Idol phase. His hair was blond and spiky, although not as bleached as that of the peroxide pop star himself. Like a million other teenagers, Ewan ignored protests from his father about the spikiness of his haircut—Jim had been getting complaints from other teachers who thought it should be toned down a little.

Ewan and Vicky had been friends for some time when they started going out together, but within six weeks it was all over—after he found her smoking an experimental cigarette with friends at the side of a tennis court. His annoyed reaction seems strange given that he had been a smoker for some time.

"I think we started going out together because one of Ewan's friends, Crawford McBride, was seeing one of my pals," recalls Vicky, now married with two young children. "We did a lot together as a foursome and maybe it seemed appropriate to make it official. But I don't think we were meant to be. We didn't seem to have much in common. He liked Billy Idol, and I was into Bob Marley and reggae music."

By the time Ewan McGregor left school and Crieff behind for Kirkcaldy, in his newly-acquired light green Volkswagen Beetle, complete with bucket seats, he was developing into a handsome young man. At 5 feet 10½ inches tall, and mature beyond his years, he was bound to impress at least some of the 19 girls in his new class. His parents were relaxed about him living away from home, and sent him to Fife not with unrealistic expectations, but sound common-sense advice that would hopefully help him cope with the challenges that lay ahead. Released for the first time from the restrictive surroundings of Crieff, he was ready for a new adventure. In a class who were together for most of the day, and tended to socialise with each other rather than mingle with those on other courses, friendships developed quickly.

It was at this time that he experienced his first sexual encounter. In one magazine interview, McGregor admitted to being apprehensive for quite some time about losing his virginity. When he finally did, he recalled that it was a wonderful experience. "I just hadn't done it, and I didn't know quite what it was about," he said. "[Then] somebody took hold of me and gave me a good one. It felt great. I felt pretty good about it."

McGregor told the interviewer that his more experienced partner was older than he, although not by much. His friend Paul Kininmonth recalled that Ewan was involved with four girls on his course—there were three short relationships, soon after the start of the first term, and one serious one.

"Ewan was a great guy, who was very much the Valentino of the class," said Kininmonth. "I think girls chased him quite a bit. If he was interested he would go for it. Other guys in the class tried and generally failed. We were envious of how well Ewan did."

Such encounters might have been expected to create tension in class, but this never happened. "Ewan was open enough about who he was seeing, but he was clever enough to not let it get out of hand," said Kininmonth. "He would always finish something, and didn't get into a situation where problems may have developed."

McGregor saw Lisa Maclennan, who shared a flat with three other girls on the course, for about a month shortly after the start of the course. "Because of the nature of our class," said one classmate, "everyone became very close. I think there weren't too many romances because we all became close friends quite quickly. We were together all the time. It kind of got past the stage where people would go out with each other. They had become too friendly. Most of the guys were nice, and Ewan didn't stand out as any kind of hunk.

He was very popular because he was a very nice guy. I don't think the girls thought he was fantastically good-looking."

Three months into the course, and after breaking up with Lisa Maclennan, Ewan became involved with another classmate, Hannah Titley, and their relationship blossomed into love almost immediately. This time it was serious. The couple may have taken a little time to find each other, but when they did, friends said they were inseparable. "They were very, very together," remembered Kininmonth. "When the course finished they were still going out, and I think some people were saying it was a marriage case."

Hannah, from London, was seventeen, the same age as McGregor. She was the only one of the 26 students who wanted a career in stage management rather than acting. He was initially attracted by her strikingly pretty face, and permed shoulder-length dark hair. Their attachment explained why the aspiring actor chose to get involved in the stage management side of most of the class's productions that year, acting as Hannah's deputy when she took charge.

Their night-time haunts were the local pub, Smithy's, which had a jukebox and a pool table, and Jackie O's, a nightclub whose cheap drink promotions attracted hordes of students on Thursday nights. When Ewan was single, he would go to the disco, not necessarily with the intention of finding female company, but certainly available if the right girl was interested, according to Kininmonth.

When he was with Hannah, however, it was an entirely different story. The pair of them were constantly holding hands, giggling with each other, revelling in the joys of their first major relationship. They were young, and deeply in love. Though strong and authoritative in class, she softened in Ewan's company according to friends, who speak affectionately of their willingness to mingle with others on the course, but always as a couple.

"Theirs was the only serious relationship on our course," said another classmate. "Remember they were only seventeen and people at that age are bound to think their relationship is the big one. They always do. Some people thought the sound of wedding bells wouldn't be far away. Had you seen them at the time, you could have believed it. But they were still so young."

Their relationship was not without problems, however. At one party, as the strains of Deacon Blue's "Real Gone Kid" filled the room, McGregor's earlier brief liaison with Maclennan cast a shadow over proceedings. "There was a bit of a bust-up because Lisa had come back on the scene for a little bit," said Kininmonth. "Lisa and Hannah were both at this party but didn't fight over him or anything like that. They just kept well apart for the night, both annoyed with each other. But it was a relatively minor hiccup."

The other lads in the class seemed to offer little competition when it came to girls, generally managing to avoid getting involved in relationships. Which is not to say they led a dull existence: one spent most of his time growing cannabis in his room. Another, said to be the least popular drama student, opened his bedroom door one night in the halls to be confronted by what appeared to be the Kirkcaldy wing of the Ku Klux Klan. He barely had time to focus on the group of boys with paper bags over their heads, before he was dragged kicking and screaming to one of the communal toilets. Once inside, the noisy crowd unceremoniously dumped him into a bath full of freezing water. The suspects—who, according to warden Tom Lawrence, included McGregor— were given a dressing down the following day by another warden, Carol Humbert. Following the stern lecture, Lawrence was asked if he had anything to say.

"Listen lads," he piped up, looking grimly round the room. "Next time you are thinking of pulling a stunt like that, come and talk to me about it beforehand. Because I want to see it too."

Lawrence called McGregor and his fellow students the "drama patients", because he thought some of them were not quite right in the head. He liked Ewan, though, re-membering him as a well-mannered, bright, down-to-earth, outgoing teenager who often returned with his best mate Andy Milarvie drunk from a night out at Jackie O's. "I remember they both appeared at my door one night, and Ewan kept repeating: 'I'm pissed, I'm pissed.' " said Lawrence, who did not hesitate to evict other students for more serious misdemeanours. "Having a drink was the kind of thing a normal boy of his age would do from time to time. He was a lovely lad, and there was no bullshit from him."

As the nine months in Kirkcaldy drew to a close, Ewan and Hannah were closer than ever but, as they were destined to go their separate ways in a few months' time, neither was sure they had a future together. He hoped to continue his studies in London, while Hannah was intending to complete her stage management training in Edinburgh.

It meant they would be 400 miles apart, leading vastly different lives. During a party at Lynn Bains' home to celebrate the completion of the course, the couple contemplated their next move. After much soul-searching, they agreed their relationship was too important to be allowed to slip away. They pledged to stay together.

The course at Kirkcaldy ended without any formal graduation ceremony, merely an assurance that their Higher National Certificates would be sent out in the post. On the last day, McGregor walked from the Beveridge Suite in the Adam Smith Theatre, the site of most of the hard work of the previous nine months, and joined his classmates for a final drink in the town's Wheatsheaf pub.

Paul Kininmonth remembered how a few of the lads gathered together behind the theatre where they had often gone for a smoke during breaks. Someone produced a guitar, and they sang a couple of songs from their own production, *A Few From The Fridge*. "At the end, I remember Ewan gave me a big hug, said 'see you Paul,' and he was off. We lived in each other's pockets yet it all came to an end so suddenly. I think we had realised by that point, though, that we were going our separate ways and that was it."

The rest of the class may have been drifting apart, but Ewan and Hannah were determined this would not happen to them. He loved her, but deep down probably knew that the career he had always dreamed of was ultimately more important. As he packed his bags for the bright lights of London, he must have wondered if their relationship was strong enough to survive.

VI

LONDON CALLING

Ewan McGregor glanced nervously at his watch. It was almost time. His friend Andy Milarvie was sitting beside him. He was just as nervous.

They were in London, at the Royal Academy of Dramatic Arts. Both had applied to get in to Britain's most prestigious drama school. Both had been granted an interview. They knew this was their big chance.

As the seconds ticked away, McGregor quietly rehearsed the speeches Uncle Denis had helped him prepare. Finally, his name was called. This was it, he thought. If he wasn't ready now, he never would be. He was confident. He was going to get in.

McGregor walked into the room and found himself facing a middle-aged tutor. As he got ready to do the audition, the tutor suggested they have a chat first.

McGregor sat down, confused.

"Now, how old are you," inquired the tutor.

"I'm seventeen," replied the would-be actor. "But I'll be eighteen by the start of the course."

"Oh well, you've got a good few years of auditions ahead of you then."

McGregor was dumbfounded. Before his audition had even started, it was over. He went through his prepared speeches, but the tutor was clearly uninterested—his mind was already made up. McGregor could see the man scribbling on a pad, and he knew what it meant: Rejection.

Minutes later he left RADA, disappointed and angry.

"Ewan was rejected because of his age, nothing else," said one friend. "The tutor was bored, miserable, and appeared to pay little attention to his pieces. He had been so fired up and excited about the audition, but went away with his heart on the floor. It was incredibly upsetting for him. He hated the bureaucracy that dismissed him because of his age, not his talent. It is still a topic he feels passionately about today."

Almost ten years later, McGregor jokingly recalled this episode during a rare television interview with Michael Parkinson.

"This is great, this is the first time I've ever got my own back on RADA," he said, warming to the task. McGregor described the incident and told how the train fare to London cost £60, and the interview itself around £30. It was a lot of money for a penniless student. Years later, he had neither forgiven nor forgotten what had happened at RADA.

McGregor and Milarvie went back to Scotland disappointed. But, as it turned out, the boy from Crieff wasn't far away from succeeding in his ambition to study drama in London. Shortly after his return, the Guildhall School of Music and Drama, one of the country's leading training colleges, granted him an interview.

Before finishing his studies in Kirkcaldy, he had attended a preliminary half-day audition with 700 other hopefuls, taking part in a movement and improvisation class before doing his three speeches. He was even asked to sing a song. Then the lecturers grilled him to find out if he had what it takes to succeed, that indefinable something that would set him apart from the other applicants.

"You need to weed out at that stage the people who just like to dabble in drama," said senior acting teacher Kenneth Rea. "You are looking for that quality that can engage you, weave a spell over you, almost instantly. It's very hard to do in a three-minute speech. When you are seeing hundreds of people it is quite rare. Very good ones stand out immediately."

One hundred students were invited back for a final audition lasting more than two days. Ewan McGregor was one of them, and this time he was tested more thoroughly. Some students were asked to recite a Shakespeare soliloquy as if they were constructing a bomb or chatting with a lover in a restaurant. At one point, McGregor was even asked to portray an elastic band. His improvisation was impressive, and when the staff gathered to pick the 26 successful candidates, he was one of the first to be chosen. "Ewan didn't have any trouble getting into Guildhall," said one staff member.

"Those who get in may be raw but we are interested in their potential," commented Rea. "We hardly expect them to be the finished product when they arrive. Other colleges may be looking for a more polished product."

The audition process had impressed McGregor far more than the one at RADA. And when a letter arrived informing him of his selection, he was ecstatic.

Early in the summer of 1989, at the end of the Kirkcaldy course, Ewan and Hannah moved in together. She had won a place on a stage management course at Edinburgh's Queen Margaret College, and rented a flat in the city's Marchmont area.

As most of Britain's aspiring actors descended on Edinburgh for the city's annual Festival, Ewan McGregor quietly made some extra money to help fund his move to London. He worked for £2.50 an hour at the Gennaro Pizzeria in the Grassmarket, where he struck up a friendship with waiter Paolo Diotaiuti. "It was just a summer job but he had a good laugh with customers, especially women," said Diotaiuti. "They always left good tips." By this time the young McGregor who had modelled himself on Billy Idol was long gone, replaced by a laid-back teenager sporting a longer, more wavy hairstyle. "He looked like a yuppie," added his waiter pal.

Ewan became more self-assured and mature as he grew

closer to Hannah. She often turned up at the restaurant near to closing time when her boyfriend was on a late shift, and Diotaiuti was struck by how close they seemed. For three months the couple lived for each other, cooking together some evenings and, although money was tight, even taking in the odd Festival show.

But summer had to end. When McGregor walked out of the flat for the last time to go to London, they vowed to keep their relationship going—by phone, letter and the occasional visit. Faced with being 400 miles apart, they remained staunchly committed to staying close. "They were deeply in love with each other," said one friend. "It was a completely natural thing to do and they both believed their relationship was strong enough."

Those phone calls became a regular occurrence as he adapted to the shock of living in England's capital. It was a world away from anything he had experienced before. Crieff had a population of 6,000, Kirkcaldy about 50,000 and London more than seven million. The sheer size of the sprawling metropolis overwhelmed the boy from the Highlands. To see green fields, he now faced a two-hour journey. Everywhere he went there were crowds of people, at all hours of the day, and for an impoverished student the high cost of living came as a real shock.

McGregor was also struck by sights he had never seen before. There were no beggars in Crieff, but in London there were thousands. At the other end of the spectrum, he saw at first hand the heady excesses of the yuppie-fuelled "loadsamoney" culture of the late 1980s. These extremes were equally alien for a teenager struggling to come to terms with his new life in London.

McGregor's first home in the capital was a spartan room at a YMCA hostel in the heart of the city's financial district. It acted as an unofficial hall of residence for the Guildhall school just a few minutes' walk down the road.

"He found it really hard at first, but everyone does," remarked one friend, who also said Ewan's parents and Hannah were hugely supportive whenever he phoned home seeking reassurance. "Anyone of that age is going to find a place like London difficult to settle into, especially when you come from a wee place like Crieff. Living on his own in the YMCA didn't make it any better. He was really fending for himself. But Ewan was cut out for challenges, he wasn't one for shirking them. He wasn't keen on the place at first. That's for sure. But Ewan was very positive because of his excitement at getting on to the course. He was so determined to do well on it."

The YMCA was hardly ideal as a home, but was only a short walk to the college. Guildhall, though, was not a pretty sight. It was situated within the Barbican Centre, an ugly modern complex in London's financial district. Arguably one of the most hideous pieces of architecture of recent times, it was a drab brown concrete jungle with a maze of walkways and tunnels that was impossible not to get lost in. And tucked away in a small corner of this urban citadel was the prestigious centre of dramatic excellence.

At Guildhall McGregor was faced with a three-year vocational course designed to challenge the students. The first year focused primarily on teaching certain skills, which the students went on to use in a series of small internal productions in the following year. One of the highlights of second year was a tour around Europe—including Istanbul and Hamburg—during which McGregor played Orlando in a production of *As You Like It*. "That boosted my confidence quite a lot because I had always been scared of Shakespeare." By the final year the students were considered to be almost fully trained, and their efforts were directed towards the annual showcase for casting directors and agents.

Just as in Kirkcaldy, the hours were long—often from nine in the morning until seven at night, with lines to learn afterwards. But the training was far more challenging. The Guildhall philosophy was to dissect each young artist's talent into tiny pieces, then reassemble it in a markedly different fashion. It was a process many students found stressful, and some simply could not cope. They were put through the mill in a thorough programme that concentrated on everything from voice techniques to stage fighting. Rea emphasised that Guildhall provided a classical training for the theatre of tomorrow. The students were encouraged to open up and express themselves. Then the staff would examine their abilities in minute detail.

"I tell them that although we will give them skills, once we start to work on them we will also take something away. So they must be very clear about their identity, beliefs and ideals after they begin training. They may find out they are not as good as they thought, and that can be a major upheaval to their identity. Take that away and they have nothing. We always make it clear we feel there's something special about them. That has to be kept alive throughout. The training is very hard, and challenging and exposing. We're very supportive, though. We don't want to demolish a student, but we do want to challenge them to get the very best out of their talent."

The combination of a strange, new environment and tough teaching methods took its toll on Ewan McGregor, and he struggled initially. Indeed, one of his first experiences at Guildhall left him doubting his ability to make the grade. At the beginning of the first term, a lecturer asked the latest intake to share their life stories. One by one, each recounted the kind of terrible experiences McGregor had only read about in newspapers. His mind reeled as tales of evil, destruction and all the worst things that can be possibly be inflicted on human beings were described in harrowing detail by his fellow students.

"I didn't seem to have any," said McGregor, who had drawn a blank trying to remember if he had encountered any mad axe murderers up The Knock. "I was going, Fuck it. I'm never going to make it. I'm obviously not of the right stock. I didn't suffer enough."

In one interview, he later recalled how much the teaching methods initially sapped his confidence and left him feeling self-conscious. He said the most valuable thing he learned during his time at Guildhall was getting used to living in London. "I always thought I was fantastic until I got to drama school, where that notion was soundly thrashed out," he said. "I don't know if college can teach you to be a great actor."

Rea understood perfectly why students often had negative opinions of their drama school days. "There are things you are taught at drama school which you may not see the point of till years afterwards," he said. "That's typical of student actors' memories. There are bound to be things they won't understand at the time."

He also acknowledged the enormous pressures placed on the students. "Some of them are away from home for the first time. In a new city it is very difficult for someone who is still a teenager. That's why people who are a bit older perhaps have a better chance of adjusting."

For some people, however, drama school was more of a hindrance than a help. As the actor Robert Carlyle commented on his time at the Royal Academy of Music and Drama in Glasgow: "It took me at least four years to get rid of the garbage they had put in. Drama school is all about compartmentalising people and turning them into actors in a conveyor-belt sort of way. There is a terrible generalisation in the way they teach. Drama schools are incestuous and insular places. You are analysing the wrong stuff because you are looking at each other. Life is what you should be looking at."

McGregor's experiences of Guildhall were more positive, but the first year was still a stressful time, and he turned to Hannah for reassurance. They spent hours on the phone, and wrote often. Some weekends he travelled back to Scotland, and others Hannah went down south. For months their relationship remained strong.

But at the end of his first year in London it was clear they were growing apart. The distance involved was putting their relationship under strain. Hardly surprising, as they were living totally separate lives.

Ewan had formed his own circle of friends in London, and Hannah hers in Edinburgh. Finally they decided it was time to go their separate ways. One friend remembers the split being completely amicable. "They had a good thing going together but people change and move on," he said. "And they were wise enough to realise that was the right time to do it. It had become too much for both of them to pursue their careers and each other at the same time. It was a mutual decision, and it was good for them at the time because it allowed them both space. They remain close friends now."

Ewan also had to dig deep for cash during his college days. Jim and Carol lived a comfortable lifestyle in Crieff, and helped their son out when they could. But their teachers' salaries were not enough to ensure him an easy financial ride through his studies.

He was forced to sell his beloved Volkswagen Beetle to raise extra cash, and friends recalled him being broke most of the time. With his college pal Zubin Varla, he busked at a nearby tube station and played in a restaurant on Sundays, under the name Mano et Mano.

And yet the longer Ewan stayed in London, the more he

came to like it. After spending his first year living at the YMCA, he moved to a flat on the notorious Kingsmead housing estate on the edge of Hackney Marsh. The flat was one of hundreds in a run-down collection of tower blocks, in an area that had one of the highest crime rates in London. "I liked it there," recalled McGregor. "It was weird. Apparently it is the big dangerous one, but I didn't see any trouble there." Later he lived in another flat in Hackney, before moving in with students in a flat in the east London district of Leytonstone.

Although he may have had misgivings about the course, on balance he appeared to enjoy his two and a half years there. "He said he learnt a lot at Guildhall, and had a whale of a time," said one friend. "When he went there he was cocky as shit. He had been one of 26 people picked from 700 to get into this course, and he thought he was one of the best actors in the world. And then he realised that every one of these other 25 actors thought they were the best in the world too. He was always confident he was good, but when he got there he realised he had so much to learn. It was a hard process, but I think he appreciated it."

At the start of the course McGregor had been worried that an actor needed to experience suffering to succeed. But later, after winning critical acclaim for his portrayal of crazed junkie Mark Renton in *Trainspotting*, he was dismissive of those initial fears. "Now it just annoys me," he said. "Actors that feel they have to suffer; that everything has to come from a point of pain. Fuck off."

By early 1992 McGregor was doing well in his third year. College had been tough, but staff noticed that his natural talent had benefited greatly from the rigorous training. They were also confident that he would stand out in the crucial final year showcase in front of about two hundred casting agents and directors.

When McGregor finally walked out on to the stage in front of the audience that could potentially make or break his career, he belted out a Barbara Streisand song, before launching into an extract from the film *Withnail & I* and finishing off with his own version of "Lean On Me". But by that point he was sure he had bombed.

McGregor's performance had also included his own piece about an oil worker who lost his legs in an accident on a rig. Midway through the scene his mind went blank, his lines forgotten. The audience watched as he paused, then looked down to rub his stump. He raised his head again, regained his composure and carried on. But by then he thought the damage had been done. "I came off and thought, 'Fuck, that's it, I've blown it.'"

However, far from having blown it, he had caused quite a stir.

"Ewan attracted a lot of interest," said one staff member. "He was good. He always had a very strong presence and a very good rapport with audiences. A lot of that is to do with attitude. To project a warmth and generosity that reaches out to the audience, but not in an over-confident way, makes you more attractive."

"A lot of casting directors are quite ruthless in what they look for," said Kenneth Rea. "Talent as an actor is not necessarily all they want. Of course that is important. But they might look more immediately for someone who is going to be what they call 'commercial'. That means they can make a lot of money out of that person. Someone who will look good on television, for instance, rather than an all-round actor. Good-looking young people will be cast more easily. The people you consider to be the most interesting actors won't necessarily get the best roles."

After the performance McGregor was approached by Lindy King, an agent who said she was interested in talking to him about the possibility of a forthcoming TV role. It was just what he wanted to hear.

"He went to drama school not to become a good drama student, but to become a good actor," said a friend. "That's why when the chance arose to get out early, he did. He's always been very determined. He has never wavered from his goal."

As the inexperienced young drama student prepared to leave Guildhall, he could hardly have imagined what lay ahead of him. Going into television straight from college usually involved a minor role in an insignificant production. But for McGregor it was different—he was about to get the chance of a lead role in a major series.

VII

Presley, Potter & Stendhal

On a cold night in early 1992, Ewan McGregor could have been forgiven if he was seized by a strong sense of *déjà vu*. In a strange woman's flat he found himself going through routines mastered years earlier in his own living-room. He could almost hear the encouraging voice of his father. . . .

"C'mon, Ewan," Jim had shouted. "Give us a bit of *Hound Dog*." Jim turned to his friend, and whispered: "Just watch this. He might be young but he's really good."

The needle on the turntable moved into position, and the old vinyl record crackled. Then the voice of the king of rock 'n' roll filled the room.

At the same time Ewan McGregor raised himself on to his

toes, ready to move. He looked towards his audience and, with perfect timing, opened his mouth as Elvis opened his.

Jim, Carol and their friends watched young Ewan, by now in full swing. When the record came to an end, the adults burst into enthusiastic applause. Ewan took a quick bow, then darted off his stage, feeling justifiably pleased with himself. Not a bad performance for a five-year-old.

And now here he was—jiving, grooving and miming his way into the world of TV. He hoped his performance was substantially more polished these days.

Television producer Rosemarie Whitman had been searching for months for a young actor who could act, dance, sing and, most important of all, lip-sync—the Achilles' heel of every would-be pop star. On a comfortable sofa, she sat with choreographer Quinny Sacks watching the gyrating McGregor dance his heart out. Moments earlier that same heart had been pumping twice as fast as he waited nervously for his big audition.

McGregor would never have been there at all if Lindy King had not been at the Guildhall showcase. It was there that she had spotted McGregor and loved him. All too aware that the producers of a forthcoming TV series were having problems filling one of the leading parts, she approached the show's casting director Lucy Boulting. "We had been told he was wonderful and that we had to see him," said Whitman. "But agents always say things like that. It was the eleventh hour and I was seeing this student who had not even graduated yet."

Ewan McGregor's biggest moment to date was taking place in a studio on the top floor of Sacks' London flat. With the volume on the stereo system turned up loud, the unmistakable voice of Elvis Presley filled the room, as Whitman watched, stunned.

"He's amazing," she thought, before turning to Sacks and winking approvingly. McGregor was concentrating too hard on his moves to notice.

"I knew I had found the man," Whitman recalled. "We sat there and thought he was just brilliant. I had read alongside him just before when he was fantastic. But we had had tremendous difficulty filling this part because we needed someone who could dance and lip-sync, which is extraordinarily difficult. If you don't get it spot on you blow the convention. I just sat there watching him."

Whitman reached forward, and took a sip from a glass of wine. She sat back, and let out a huge sigh of relief.

"Thank God for that," she thought. Her marathon search was over.

The following day she phoned the programme makers at Channel 4, and said: "We have got this fantastic young man. We have got to go for him now."

They trusted her instincts, and McGregor had won his first big part. As he toasted the news with champagne, he could have been forgiven for muttering Long Live The King.

That night in London, fate had smiled on the boy from Crieff. Plucked from obscurity, he was about to play a leading role in *Lipstick on Your Collar*, celebrated playwright Dennis

Potter's new television series. It was a remarkable achievement—to top the bill in a major TV show straight from college was almost unheard of. The producers were so sure of their choice that McGregor wasn't even required to do a screen test—it would have clashed with his final college production, and they were happy to let him proceed with that instead.

As McGregor flicked through the *Lipstick* script over the festive season, he noticed the enormous number of times his character appeared. It was a daunting prospect, even for a young man whose confidence knew few bounds. All his classmates from Guildhall would have been envious of his first job, but some believed he had bitten off more than he could chew, and a few quietly hoped he would fall flat on his face. Perhaps only now did McGregor realise the sheer scale of the production he had become involved in. But despite the fears and doubts, there was no way he could turn his back on such a marvellous opportunity.

In early March, a few weeks before his course was due to finish, McGregor left Guildhall for the last time. He had no regrets—the course tutors actively encouraged students to find jobs during their final year. Even so, they were surprised when they heard where he was going. They had seen students in the past winning secondary roles in TV shows, but never a lead part as prestigious as this.

Lipstick on Your Collar was scheduled to take seven months to shoot, primarily at London's Twickenham Studios, but also on location around the city, and at Pinewood Studios in

Buckinghamshire. It was to be shown in six one-hour episodes the following year on Channel 4, the latest in a trilogy of musical dramas from the writer regarded by some as a shock artist, and by others as Britain's foremost playwright. Potter's highly ambitious and critically acclaimed series *The Singing Detective*, set in the 1930s, had outraged conservative-minded viewers—one explicit sex scene in particular sparked howls of protest and acres of newspaper coverage. As a result, all of Potter's future offerings would be acclaimed by his supporters and derided by his enemies.

Lipstick is a black comedy set against the backdrop of Britain in the mid-1950s, dragging itself out of the post-Second World War depression, only to drift into the humiliation of the Suez crisis. It tells the story of a young Welshman, Private Francis Francis, and his experiences in military intelligence. His mate—McGregor's character, Private Mick Hopper—is a bored Russian translator conscripted into the War Office. An aspiring drummer, he represents the new generation of malcontents, inspired by rock 'n' roll, who are in conflict with the staid officer-class who see their own identity threatened by the crumbling of the British Empire. In the series Potter made use of fantasy musical sequences— his trademark device—as Hopper whiles away the six weeks to his demobilisation by imagining himself and his colleagues singing and jiving to the latest rock 'n' roll hits such as Elvis's *Don't Be Cruel* or Frankie Vaughan's *Green Door*.

The shoot began in March 1992, and Ewan quickly realised the hours were even longer in the real world. He was on a five day/six-day schedule that often involved wake-up calls as early as 5 a.m., and a driver outside his door an hour later to take him to work. He had arrived on set a spotty 20-year-old with fair hair, but in no time his hair, eyebrows and eyelashes were jet black for the part, and his complexion was revitalised by a series of facials.

"He was very scruffy when he arrived," recalled make-up-artist Sally Jay. "He was all mousey and spotty so we did a bit of a transformation. We got the hair curlers on his head, the face packs on and he loved it. He had lots of different looks throughout the series, like wearing wigs when he was Elvis, so sometimes he had some pretty lengthy make-up sessions."

On one occasion, during a bedroom scene, McGregor lifted his arms above his head to reveal blond hairs in his armpit. Filming was brought to a halt as the offending strands were quickly dyed black.

When the time came for the Elvis sequences he had no problems. "Doing him was extraordinarily easy because I had spent most of my childhood pretending to be Elvis Presley. I just suddenly felt like Elvis, it was great." Impersonating Gene Vincent, however, proved a little more tricky. "I was really terrified when I did Gene Vincent because there were all these people from a 1950s club who came along to be extras and they kept shouting, 'nah, nah, that's not right!' It was bad enough having to do all this lip-syncing for the cameras and acting at the same time, never mind getting crits from everyone in the audience. It was good fun though."

The four leading characters in the series were in their late teens or early twenties, so the actors cast to play them had to be young, a big factor in the decision to give McGregor his chance. His three co-stars, Giles Thomas (Francis), Louise Germaine (Sylvia) and Kimberley Huffman (Lisa), were equally inexperienced, and had never before been tested in such demanding roles. The producers knew casting them was a risk—but an unavoidable one. As it turned out, the gamble paid off, and the young quartet acquitted themselves admirably. Typically, McGregor was making the most of the opportunity—others noticed how he kept a close eye on all aspects of the production and, just as in Perth, his inquisitive nature came to the fore as he sought advice from experienced actors like Peter Jeffrey.

For the young Scot it was also a defining moment in his relationship with his parents. They arrived at Twickenham Studios one day to see their son—who had left school with hope and not much else—at the centre of a huge TV production. Their hearts filled with pride as Dennis Potter treated them to a slap-up meal. When Ewan had left school four years earlier, he had done so with the nagging feeling that he had let his parents down. Perhaps, on this day, in the company of Potter, he finally rid himself of those doubts.

"It was so important for him that they saw him doing well," said one friend. "He had never forgotten the faith they had shown in him. I think he felt *Lipstick* was proof, if you like, that they were right to show that faith. He was determined to succeed, but it meant so much for him to believe his parents thought that way as well."

"When his parents came to the set, you could see they were really proud of him," said Sally Jay, who remembered McGregor being confident, but polite and charming. Rosemarie Whitman noticed the same attributes. "He was remarkable, they all were," she said. "Ewan arrived a young, naive but confident man. He was incredibly professional on set, and performed so maturely in such a demanding role. He did not play about, he did not waste the experience. The great thing about *Lipstick* is that it really showed him off. He also chatted to Dennis a lot. He was respectful of Dennis because of how well he was regarded, but never in awe of him. He was just himself. Louise was like that as well. I think Dennis appreciated that. He found it refreshing, and had a lot of laughs with them."

The Hopper role was high-profile, but it was only the first rung on the ladder, and it would be a long time before McGregor started commanding fees he could live off comfortably. The four youngsters were paid far less than their more experienced counterparts—their pay packets are believed to have barely reached five figures. This caused no animosity, though—they viewed *Lipstick* as a great learning experience. Indeed, Whitman remembered the set as one of the friendliest she had worked on. The youngsters, free from cynicism or backbiting, often went to the pub together after a hard day's work, and some remained friends afterwards.

On March 31 the rest of the crew presented Ewan with a cake in the shape of a guitar to celebrate his 21st birthday. Just like his character in the show, he could have been forgiven for believing it was all a dream. Of the other students at his college—including Neil Morrissey of *Men Behaving Badly* fame, or comedian Alistair McGowan—no-one had come so far in such a short time.

It may have taken the viewing public, and the critics, a little longer to notice his considerable talent, but McGregor's performance as the bored Hopper was impressive for a beginner. He looked back on *Lipstick* as a valuable first experience of how a large TV production actually worked. Until then he had been unsure of the practicalities of acting in front of cameras, and he watched closely, picking up knowledge that would prove invaluable. But his personal experience with Potter also left a lasting impression. So great was his admiration for the controversial writer that he made a brief appearance in Potter's final work, *Karaoke*, which was made after the writer's death from cancer. By that time McGregor did not need to do it, but he wanted to, as a tribute.

"He'd talk to me and warn me about what might happen after *Lipstick* came out, and about my responsibility to my talent," McGregor said, explaining how he once ended up being given advice by Potter late at night in a graveyard. The playwright, who was very ill at the time, intermittently disappeared behind a headstone to be sick, returning as though nothing had happened.

McGregor recognised Potter's unique talent: "I think he is a genius and although it took a while to get to know him, I really respect him. He's a brave man and had a lot of philosophical things to say about acting. He also gave me a lot of very clued-up advice."

When production on *Lipstick* finished in the autumn of 1992, Potter's army of fans were hoping that television's most imaginative writer would not disappoint them, as they waited expectantly for the first episode to be screened, on Sunday, February 21 the following year.

Sitting in his new bachelor pad in the Primrose Hill area of London, McGregor also had high hopes that instant acclaim would come his way. After all, this was his first major appearance on the small screen, and he was sure that, as with previous Dennis Potter projects, there would be a big reaction. Sadly, these high hopes were somewhat misplaced.

Despite months of work from Rosemarie Whitman and Lindy King to drum up publicity, the media's appetite for the latest Potter offering and its four young stars was almost non-existent in the run-up to the first episode. The pair worked relentlessly to generate interest from newspapers and magazines, but their efforts were to no avail. They had been sure someone would bite, but clearly the magazines forgot to read the script.

The lack of interest was infuriating. At one incredibly disappointing publicity appearance, only three people turned up. "I was so proud of these young people," said Whitman, "and I thought everything was going to be terrific. We worked for months trying to get pre-publicity and had two very pretty girls, two very pretty boys and a sexy story. They seemed to be the right ingredients but so few people seemed interested.

I didn't understand why that was the case then, and still don't now."

Things went from bad to worse when the series was engulfed in a row no-one could have predicted. The makers were left reeling when one woman wrote to a newspaper, complaining about a rape scene at the end of the first episode. The story was then seized upon by rest of the media. *Lipstick* was certainly in the news now—but for all the wrong reasons. "The director Renny Rye and I wrote a letter in reply explaining that it wasn't a rape scene at all," said Whitman. "But the whole thing got out of hand. It turned out that the woman who wrote the letter was in fact a journalist who had been put up to it by an editor. She started going on radio talk shows and it got so silly Dennis even said this woman was getting more work out of slagging off his work than she had ever got off her own bat."

The controversy merely added to the generally negative reaction to the series. Whitman said the makers were depressed by ratings of only five million viewers—although this was considered impressive for a programme on Channel 4. "We were disappointed by the reaction at the time," she added. "There was some dreadful publicity in the press against it. Maybe they decided Dennis had had his successes and they weren't going to allow him another one."

Amongst all the furore, few people picked up on the name Ewan McGregor. The critics' views on the series were mixed, but most tended to overlook McGregor's role, despite the fact he had shown great versatility. In *The Times*, Lynne Truss complained the lip-syncs failed because they were badly directed, and said Hopper's part was poorly developed. "We knew nothing about him," she protested, adding: "But Ewan McGregor was good in the part, and in fact the great all-round success of *Lipstick* is the casting." One of his former tutors was impressed. "There are always openings for young actors," he said. "I think *Lipstick* was very well directed and Ewan was good because he had the skills."

McGregor was right to be proud of his efforts on *Lipstick*. At the same time, though, he experienced a great sense of anticlimax in the period after filming finished, finding himself on the casting circuit for the best part of four months, with no offers coming his way. He found this lull hard to cope with, and even feared he might never work again.

"I dealt with it really badly and should have shut my mouth. But it's like anything: you're the one living this thing, so if you're pissed off at the time, you're pissed off. And you'll always think you'll never work again."

Things did not improve much when the first episode eventually went on air. "I was waiting for six months for it to come out," he said, "looking at the date in my calendar, and I really, truly believed that the day after the first episode came out my life would be changed. [But] it's telly. It's there for an hour and then it's gone."

At that point, McGregor resigned himself to waiting a little longer before making his mark properly. He had been exposed to the viewing public for the first time, not just as an actor, but as a singer, dancer and karaoke king all at the same

time. He knew he was good. Sadly, few viewers even remembered his name.

Jim McGregor, however, was most impressed. "It was
funny to see him when he gets up on the desk in a gold suit
and does Elvis," he said. "I've been seeing him do that since
he was a wee boy."

And Ewan's fear of never working again soon evaporated.
After *Lipstick*, he spent a month in Morocco, appearing as an
extra in a major feature film. A few months later, in the New
Year of 1993, he landed a role in a stage play.

Then came the audition which would re-establish his
confidence, and advance his career to new heights. The BBC
were planning an epic new costume drama based on the
classic French novel *Le Rouge et Le Noir* by Stendhal. Of
prime importance was their search for a dashing, handsome
young actor to play the story's swashbuckling hero.

McGregor came away from the first audition convinced he
had failed to make the right impression. But director Ben
Bolt and producer Ros Wolfes knew star quality when they
saw it, and McGregor was their man.

Wolfes just wanted to see him on screen, in order to be
absolutely sure. She picked up the phone, called Rosemarie
Whitman, and asked for an extract from *Lipstick*.

"We've had Ewan in, he's magnificent, but I've got to see
him on screen," Wolfes told Whitman.

Whitman was happy to oblige, and sent over a clip of
McGregor doing a rock 'n' roll number.

"It was completely different from what we were going to

be doing," recalled Wolfes. "But Ewan was marvellous on screen. We knew he would be right for our part."

McGregor returned for a second meeting thinking he would really have to impress if he was to win the role. He had no idea it was already his.

VIII

SCARLET PRIDE

The small French town was in turmoil, the streets packed for the arrival of the King. Amid the roar of cannon, the Royal escort rode by, resplendent in all their finery. Among them was Julien Sorel, who, catching sight of Madame de Renal in the throng that pressed all around him, reared his horse on to its hind legs in an attempt to impress her. But in doing so he lost his balance, slipped from the saddle and slammed into the ground. As the dust settled, several members of the film crew raced to the scene. Ewan McGregor was already back on his feet.

"I'm all right, I'm all right," he said. "I can do this. I know I can. I'll get it next time. Let me try again."

His producer Ros Wolfes looked at director Ben Bolt, who looked at stunt co-ordinator Terry Forrestel. He assured them there was no problem—McGregor had done it that morning, and Forrestel was sure he could do it now.

Ros Wolfes turned to the actor, who was brushing himself down. "OK, Ewan, but be careful. The last thing we need is you hurt."

McGregor climbed back on the horse and rode back to his starting point. The extras were once again told to prepare for the big scene.

"OK, Action," shouted Ben Bolt.

Again McGregor rode towards the cameras, pulling the horse on to its hind legs. The result was the same, only this time he fell more awkwardly, as the horse came crashing down partly on top of him. The crew rushed over to find the young actor nursing a twisted knee.

"Are you OK Ewan?" asked Wolfes.

"Oh yeah, I'm fine. I'm sure I can do this. One more time."

McGregor may have wanted to try again, but Wolfes was worried. She looked at the stunt co-ordinator and then shook her head. They were only a few weeks into filming and any further injury to their leading man would be disastrous.

"I'm sorry Ewan, we can't afford to risk it."

It was always going to be a tricky scene, and when the cameras rolled, McGregor had been unable to master it. His hours of practice had proved in vain. Disconsolately, he walked away as a stuntman took his place. "I felt terrible about telling him he couldn't do it," said Ros Wolfes. "But I didn't want our hero injured. When he watched the proceedings from the side, he looked so deflated.

"The first time the horse just didn't react and he came off. Against my better judgment I let him try again but the stunt co-ordinator assured me it would be OK. The next time I put my foot down. Someone asked me what they would have done on *Dances With Wolves* if Costner had had problems riding. But this wasn't *Dances With Wolves*, and I wanted my lead actor back in one piece. It was an incredibly difficult scene even though Ewan was very good on a horse. Later in the filming, he had another riding scene which he handled perfectly."

McGregor was in France shooting the BBC's latest costume drama, *Scarlet and Black*. That morning he had encountered a minor setback, and his spirits were low. Ever the perfectionist, and always ready to prove people wrong, he saw himself as having failed. But those around him viewed the situation differently—if anything, they were surprised that he had been so eager to take on such a difficult scene in the first place. Other lead actors would still have been in bed, waiting to be told the stuntman had done it for them.

Ewan McGregor had been troubled by similar feelings of failure after his first meeting with *Scarlet's* producer and director four months earlier. They had already rejected his close friend Jude Law for the role of the hero, Julien Sorel, when Ewan was invited to audition by casting director Michelle Gish. Afterwards, he left their office feeling the same way as his friend. "I am very ambitious," he said later.

"I always wanted to be an actor. I took no notice of people who tried to put me off. It was the same with getting this part. The first time I went to see the director, Ben Bolt, I got the impression I wasn't what he was looking for. The second time, I was determined to make him change his mind."

But there was no need. "It was Christmas time and Ewan was like a Christmas present," said Wolfes. "He was quite nervous but we had a most enjoyable half hour with him. It was as instant as that." Wolfes and Bolt had already decided he was their man.

In the period leading up to *Scarlet*, McGregor was depressed and worried. In the six months between the completion of Lipstick and the start of filming on the post French Revolution drama, he had found work hard to come by.

"Two weeks into that and I was moping," he recalled. "And a friend said: 'What's wrong?' I said: 'I've been out of work two weeks.' And he rolled his eyes and said: 'Pull yourself together.'"

Work, however, had not completely dried up. As well as the odd voice-over for TV adverts, he had spent a month in Morocco on the set of Bill Forsyth's latest feature film, *Being Human*, starring Robin Williams.

The Scottish director had an impressive record. In the early eighties he had made two highly regarded movies, *Gregory's Girl* and *Local Hero*. In *Local Hero*, Ewan's uncle, Denis Lawson, shot to fame after a wonderfully unassuming performance as a sex-mad hotel owner trying to broker a fortune for himself—and the residents of a small fishing village—from an American oil company. After the success of these films, Hollywood lured Forsyth away from his native country. Now, with a cast headed by Williams, he was making *Being Human*, and Uncle Denis's nephew had been offered the chance to be a part of it. McGregor spent a month in Morocco, but his role was tiny. As shipwrecked Portuguese sailor Alvarez, his part amounted to a mere two lines. Indeed, the young pretender, who never saw the finished cut, always thought it was just one line—until a well-informed magazine journalist pointed out his error years later. His first line: "I'll do it, Don Paolo," was stripped to just: "I'll do it." The second came later when he informs a group of sailors who fear they are about to be eaten: "It was a joke, it was a joke."

McGregor may have had little chance to make an impression during his North African interlude, but he saw it as a marvellous opportunity to observe a major movie set in action, and each day he would watch and listen, admiring the way actors like Williams went about their business. Just by watching them rehearsing or in action, he was able to pick up invaluable tips.

Being Human is a fine movie, one of Bill Forsyth's best, but unfortunately it was not a success. Panned by the critics, it bombed at the American box-office.

In the New Year, McGregor joined an impressive cast in Joe Orton's celebrated play, *What The Butler Saw*, at the Salisbury Playhouse just outside London. Famously booed by the audience at its first production in 1969, the play had come to be regarded as a modern classic by the time McGregor landed the part of the pageboy, Nick, for an updated version in early 1993. Critics were impressed by his "amusing" performance, especially as he wobbled on high heels or appeared fully naked in front of the audience. "I had to do two streaks across the stage," remembered the actor, who insisted he had no problems with stripping off in front of a large theatre crowd. "The first time you get your clothes off you feel slightly odd. There's a moment when you drop your dressing gown . . . then you just get on with it. I couldn't wait for the moment because the Salisbury audience was a nice, solid lot and it was funny to get my kit off and wait for their reaction. To me, being on stage naked is like swimming. It feels really comfortable."

A few months later McGregor once again found himself in a state of profound undress. This time it was in front of film cameras, during the making of *Scarlet and Black*, and his audience would be rather more substantial. The three episodes of *Scarlet* were scheduled for a prime-time Sunday night slot on BBC 1 later in the year. The adaptation of Stendhal's classic 19th-century novel was part of a bold attempt by the BBC to regain its place as the producer of the finest period dramas, and win back viewers from commercial rival ITV.

Recent successes, such as a raunchy adaptation of *Lady Chatterley's Lover*, had paved the way for a more steamy adaptation of *Scarlet and Black* than readers of the novel would probably remember. In the book, Stendhal, in keeping with the conventions of his time, refers subtly to Sorel's bedroom antics: "When Julien left Madame de Renal's room a few hours later, it might be said, to adopt the language of novels, that he had nothing further left to wish for." On screen, however, little is left to the imagination, as viewers are given a graphic portrayal of the precise manner in which his wishes are realised. McGregor and actress Alice Krige, who later appeared as the Borg Queen in *Star Trek: First Contact*, thrash about naked on a carpet with the kind of spirit Stendhal could perhaps have imagined, but could never have included within the pages of his novel.

The story centres around a peasant's son, Sorel, who embarks on the relentless pursuit of power and status in the highest echelons of Parisian society. Idolising Napoleon, he sees the church and the army as the means by which he will fulfil his ambitions. Along the way, he has an affair with an older woman, Madame de Renal (Alice Krige), who is the wife of a mayor, before escaping to seduce Mathilde (Rachel Weisz), the daughter of the influential Marquis de la Mole. Mathilde becomes pregnant and goes on hunger strike after Sorel is banished by her father. Sorel is eventually executed for shooting and wounding Madame de Renal, and both love-struck ladies are left distraught by his demise.

Rachel Weisz later recalled the memorable final scene: "Ewan gets guillotined and the last shot is of my character unwrapping his head on her lap. They couldn't get a prosthetic head, so they had to cut a hole in my skirt and Ewan had to lie under the skirt for hours with his head between my legs."

The script also required McGregor to spend much of his time on the seven-week shoot completely naked. "One day I was naked the whole time," he said. "We had to film a sequence in four different places so I was just driven about in a dressing gown. At other times I was running around naked, jumping out windows carrying bundles of clothes while being shot at. I quite enjoyed it actually."

On one occasion, he attempted to persuade the director, Ben Bolt, to let him run through a French field in the nude. Bolt was worried the actor might hurt himself on rocks or glass, but McGregor would not take no for an answer. "I persuaded him. I went on and on until he agreed," he said. "And I must say, it was a very nice experience indeed."

Wolfes remembered McGregor lightened the atmosphere of nude scenes with jokes afterwards, but said he always carried out the task in a thoroughly professional manner. Clever camera angles ensured the "McGregor heirloom" made only the most fleeting appearance on *Scarlet*, but female fans were not to be disappointed as nudity would soon become a regular feature in his films. Many actors struggle with the concept of displaying their genitals on screen, but even this early in his career, and certainly ever since, McGregor has had no problems with taking his clothes off in front of the cameras. His relaxed attitude—that those scenes are fine so long as the script justifies them—has never altered. Later, when he starred in an erotic film, *The Pillow Book*, certain women's magazines went so far as to analyse the size, shape and attractiveness of his appendage. At a chance meeting, even Britain's most revered film critic, Barry Norman, wryly observed: "I see you dress to the right."

"There were a lot of nude scenes but I am not embarrassed about taking my clothes off," said McGregor after *Scarlet and Black*. "I find it really easy."

Before filming began, however, the young star suffered from the same self-doubts that he had experienced when he was reading the script of *Lipstick*—except that this time the whole thing seemed so much more daunting. Once more he feared he was in over his head. "I had a complete crisis," he said. "I suddenly felt crushed by the weight of responsibility inherent in the part, and genuinely doubted I was up to it. I was scared. But the final straw was when a fellow actor told me that, bar Hamlet, this had to be the best part for a young actor."

McGregor panicked, and a week before rehearsals were due to begin, he returned home to Perthshire seeking re-assurance. He had always been able to rely on his parents for support in times of crisis, and they did not let him down. With Carol and Jim's backing he took a deep breath, and pushed on. His fears were soon dispelled. "Once I put on my military uniform and we started filming in France everything fell into place," he said. "The uniform had an amazing effect on me. It made me feel as though I could kill someone. I just felt so powerful in it."

But *Scarlet and Black* was to be given a rough ride by the critics. *The Independent's* Thomas Sutcliffe remarked: "Ewan McGregor isn't the slight, pallid figure of the novel but a Chippendale in a frock-coat and when he encounters Madame de Renal for the first time you can almost hear the sexual excitement, like the faint crump of igniting petrol." In the *Daily Mail*, Peter Paterson commented: "It may be argued that often 20th-century actors never quite look like the characters described in 19th-century novels. That would be true, I think, of Ewan McGregor, who was far too devastatingly handsome a toy-boy figure for Julien, who is presented in the novel as a much more fragile, hesitant and socially insecure creature." The *Daily Mirror's* Simon London was less complimentary. "McGregor could have beefed up his role a bit," he wrote. "After all, Julien isn't a nice bloke—he's a scheming little git and potential home-wrecker. Yet he was played as a wet but ambitious hero." Cosmo Landesman in *The Sunday Times* was equally scathing: "As Julien, Ewan McGregor is simply too soft and too sweet. He's meant to be a young man in the grip of a demonic form of ambition, and yet he struts around looking like a young David Essex." And the *Sunday Mirror's* Joe Steeples demonstrated the hypocrisy of tabloid newspapers that thrive on stories about sex, yet complain about graphic TV programmes. "The performance by Ewan seemed short on stamina. A lack of ink in his quill, perhaps? Series like this are costly. No doubt spicy sex helps sell them round the world. But am I alone in missing the days when BBC costume drama was innocent enough for the whole family."

The viewers, however, loved *Scarlet and Black*. An audience of over 10 million confirmed its status as a hit, and created a new army of admirers for the latest star. McGregor's letterbox filled with fan-mail for the first time—mostly from housewives and star-struck teenagers.

But by this point there was another woman in his life. Since his relationship with Hannah Titley had ended, he had lived the life of an average, single, handsome, twenty-something male. There had been girlfriends, but nothing too serious. On the set of *Scarlet*, he once again fell in love.

Marie Pairis was a petite brunette who, as the production's crowd marshaller, was in charge of the huge cast of extras throughout the shoot. She had caught McGregor's eye the moment he arrived in France to start filming. The attraction was mutual and they hit it off immediately, although at first few of their colleagues realised Ewan and Marie had become more than just friends. The actor was intensely professional in his work, letting nothing get in the way, while Marie had enough on her plate co-ordinating the extras. But it wasn't long before other people on the set noticed how well they were getting on together. In local pubs and clubs, they became an item, completely inseparable before spending intimate nights in the hotel where the crew and cast were staying.

"Ewan fell madly in love," said Wolfes, "but it never got in the way of his work. I always say to actors that what they do away from the set is none of my business. But if they arrive looking hung-over, and it shows on their face, I'll take the tough schoolmistress approach with them. Ewan arrived some mornings saying he was a little bit hung-over but I never had to say anything like that to him. He was always so professional."

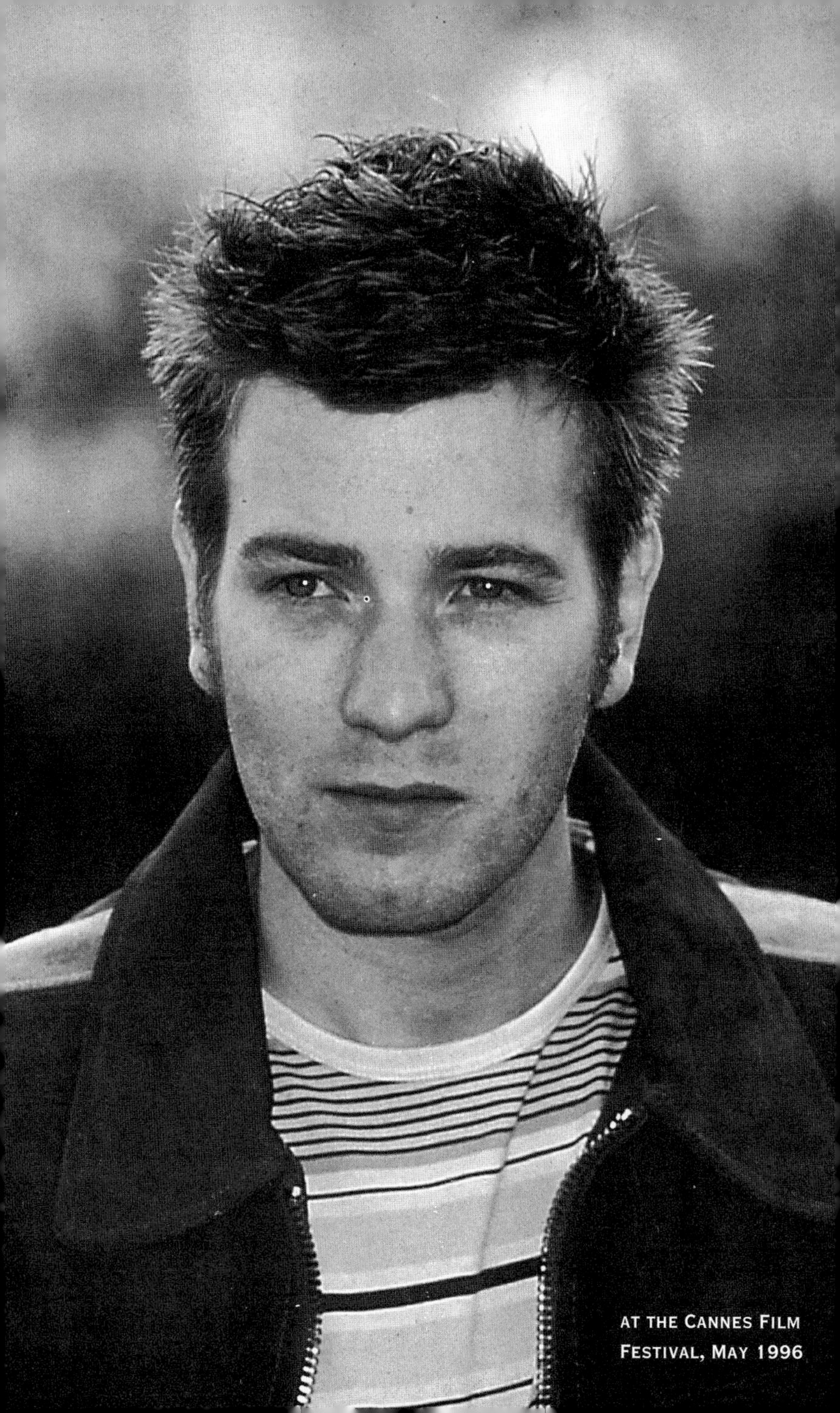

At the Cannes Film Festival, May 1996

SCHOOLDAYS 1982/3: MALCOLM COPLAND, EUAN SINCLAIR AND EWAN MCGREGOR

MORRISON'S ACADEMY 1985: EWAN MCGREGOR, MIDDLE ROW, 5TH FROM LEFT.

THE BILLY IDOL PHASE: EWAN (RIGHT), 1986

VICKY MCNALLY WITH EWAN, 1987

'SEX, VIOLENCE, EVIL, GREED, ANGER, BETRAYAL, DEATH, DISMEMBERMENT AND DISPOSAL'
SHALLOW GRAVE (1995)—ECCLESTON, FOX, MCGREGOR

'I HAD A GREAT TIME, I'VE NEVER PARTIED SO MUCH IN MY LIFE'
BLUE JUICE (1995)—PERTWEE, MACKINTOSH, GUNN, MCGREGOR

'I WAS TERRIBLE IN IT. I DIDN'T BELIEVE A WORD I SAID.'
EWAN AS FRANK CHURCHILL IN *EMMA* (1996)

THE Train

THE ACTOR   **THE PRODUCER**

spotters

THE DIRECTOR

THE WRITER

'I'M SO PROUD OF THE FILM BECAUSE I THINK WE TOLD THE TRUTH'
TRAINSPOTTING (1996)—BREMNER, MCGREGOR, CARLYLE

TRAINSPOTTING:
THE WORST TOILET
IN SCOTLAND

Wolfes noticed the young lovers growing ever closer but they never showed too much affection on set. "She was a gorgeous girl, and very sweet. They got on so well together."

In interviews to promote *Scarlet*, McGregor mentioned his girlfriend but refused to elaborate. He described the "immediate attraction" when he saw Marie, and thought the intense beginning of the relationship helped him cope with the demanding role of Julien Sorel. "I'm a romantic person," he said. "I love romantic things. I can be incredibly slushy, sometimes sickeningly so. So much of the story was about being in love and feeling passionate, so being in a position where I felt passionate anyway helped my work. Just the feeling of being in love with someone is such a powerful thing." He said he was entranced by Marie, adding: "It's providing me with huge bouts of joy and happiness."

The couple continued their relationship after filming finished by embarking on a month-long tour of the French Alps on Marie's BMW motorbike. "She's tiny as well so it must have looked very funny," said McGregor. "She was completely in charge, a real role reversal. We wore our Ray Bans and bandanas. It was like a French *Easy Rider* without the carnage."

After their touring holiday in Europe, according to a friend, the couple made a brave decision. Marie decided to give up the security of her home in France to join her boyfriend in London, where she would try and find work. Ewan, madly in love, was delighted.

He was hesitant, though, about predicting the future for

the relationship. "I don't envisage marriage and babies with anybody yet," he said.

Meanwhile, *Scarlet* was set to spark off another beautiful relationship—this time strictly professional. "I got a phone call one day from a director asking why I hadn't asked him to do *Scarlet and Black*," said Ros Wolfes. "It was Danny Boyle, and I told him he had been busy doing other things."

"OK, fine, tell me about Ewan McGregor," inquired Boyle. "I want to know all about this guy."

Danny Boyle was recruiting for his first feature film. When he heard about McGregor, he thought the young Scot would be ideal for a lead role in the movie, which would be set in his home country. The title of Boyle's film was *Shallow Grave*.

IX

DR HODGE, THE CORPSE AND THE CASH

In Bannerman's bar in Edinburgh's seedy Cowgate, two men who had never met before shook hands. Separated by a large wooden table, they sat facing each other, and quietly began to talk. One of them presented the other with a pile of hand-written notes. As his companion leafed through them, a dark and sinister tale of three flatmates, a suitcase full of money, and a dismembered corpse, began to unfold.

After half an hour, the pair shook hands again, then parted. John Hodge, a junior doctor and aspiring screenwriter, and Andrew Macdonald, a fledgling film producer, had agreed to make a movie. The meeting had been arranged by Hodge's sister, Grace, who was the sound editor on a short film Macdonald was producing for the Edinburgh Film Festival. She had pestered Macdonald until he finally agreed to read her brother's script.

On that Sunday morning in August 1991 Hodge and Macdonald were two young men whose ambition far exceeded their experience, but what they lacked in experience they more than made up for in raw talent and dogged determination—qualities that would stand them in good stead as they faced the challenges that lay ahead.

John Hodge was born in Glasgow in 1964, the son of two middle-class GPs. He went to Edinburgh Medical School when he was eighteen, but was unsure whether medicine was his true vocation. The tedium of memorising endless biochemistry tables almost forced him to quit in his first year, but Hodge plodded on, finally departing in 1987 to complete his training on the job in hospitals. By the time he returned to Edinburgh's Eastern General to sit the mandatory MRCP exam, however, he was becoming more and more disillusioned with his choice of career. It was time for a change.

During his time at university, Hodge relieved the frustration of his studies by writing film parodies for the student newspaper. In his third year he wrote the Medics' Play, *Lust for Chicken*. But it was while he was living in a crowded student flat in the city's Jeffrey Street, that he came up with the idea for a story involving a group of flatmates who find a suitcase full of money. When he finally decided to take time out from medicine to see if he could make a go of writing, this idea still lingered. After getting nowhere with a script for the TV series *Dr Findlay's Casebook*, Hodge started work on his flatmate saga.

By this time Hodge was working long hospital shifts, and would often spend a couple of hours on the latest draft when he returned home. Elements of real-life horror stories that he encountered in his hospital casualty unit provided further inspiration for the developing storyline.

At first, he tried to write a novel, but soon decided to turn it into a screenplay instead. "I just realised after writing about ten pages that I wasn't cut out to be a novelist," Hodge said later. "I still had the idea in my head, so when I came round to writing the screenplay that's what came out. It was the same story except I realised that you can't just have three twatty medical students, you've got to have a device." By the time he met Macdonald in August 1991, the crucial elements of the script that would become *Shallow Grave*—the corpse and the cash—were in place.

Born in 1966 in Glasgow, Andrew Macdonald's links with the film industry went back a long way. His grandfather was the legendary Emeric Pressburger, who had joined forces with Michael Powell to make a series of classic movies, including *The Red Shoes* and *A Matter of Life and Death*. Until he met John Hodge, Macdonald had worked in the lower echelons of the same industry on films like Hugh Hudson's *Revolution*. In 1985, he went to Los Angeles to study producing at the American Film Institute. After returning to the UK, he worked as an assistant director on *Venus Peter*, and then as location manager on a number of small British films, and the popular detective series, *Taggart*. When Hodge appeared with his notes, Macdonald was editing a short film, *Dr Reitzer's Fragment*, for the upcoming Edinburgh Film Festival.

Hodge was impressed by Macdonald at their first meeting. The producer spoke convincingly, and had an air of self-confidence. With his skinhead haircut, the writer looked mean—but he was quiet, even shy. As the script progressed, the pair formed a good working relationship, although Macdonald was not afraid of making his opinion felt—if he thought that the second half didn't work, he would let Hodge know in no uncertain terms.

As the script began to take shape, they embarked on the difficult bit—raising the money to make the film. This was where Macdonald's experience on low-budget films would prove vital. He had observed how they came together, and was all too keenly aware of the pitfalls that lay ahead. Only one thing was certain: it was not going to be easy.

Repeatedly, Hodge modified the script—dropping characters, introducing new ones, replacing whole scenes and locations, reworking the plot, and getting very little sleep until the screenplay was considered perfect. Then Macdonald would suggest yet more changes. He knew how costs could spiral out of control if any excesses were allowed to creep into the script, and he wanted each second accounted for before approaching potential backers. It was a long, hard process. A dozen rewrites and almost a year later, in July

1992, the Scottish Film Production Fund contributed £4,000 towards the project. It was a drop in the ocean, but a major breakthrough all the same. Soon afterwards, the figure was doubled to allow time for further script development. For that year's Film Festival, Macdonald, with the help of his younger director brother, Kevin, made a spoof film on how to fund a movie. Both Sean Connery and director Michael Winner appeared. It was a novel approach, but one which secured introductions to a number of major film-funders, including Channel 4. A few months later Macdonald travelled north to a conference in Inverness where he hoped to meet Channel 4's head of drama, David Aukin. Aukin was responsible for handing out roughly £700,000 to each of 12 films annually—exactly the kind of backing Macdonald was after.

At first, it all went wrong. Aukin, as it turned out, was not available. In desperation Macdonald finally managed to speak to Aukin's chauffeur. After a certain amount of persuasion, the driver accepted the script, somewhat reluctantly, and agreed to pass it on.

For the next three weeks, Macdonald heard nothing. Then, one morning in January 1993, he was dragged from his bed by an excited flatmate. The man from Channel 4 was on the phone.

Aukin liked what he had read. He was very interested, and wanted Macdonald and Hodge to meet him in London. Macdonald replaced the receiver. He was ecstatic.

On January 11, the two movie upstarts travelled south to

meet the influential TV executive. They soon discovered that Christmas had arrived late—but what a Christmas! Aukin agreed to put up £800,000 to fund their film. On the strength of this backing, the Glasgow Film Production Fund were persuaded to contribute another £150,000. A final £43,000 was coughed up by Channel 4 when detailed costs were worked out.

The dream of *Shallow Grave* had become a reality, but it had been a long haul. By the time Hodge's script was finally complete, it had been rewritten well over a dozen times— even the name had been changed, from an earlier suggestion of *Cruel*. The film was much shorter, and had a more complex plot. "Had I never met Andrew, the whole thing would never have happened," said Hodge later. All that now remained was for the film to be made. The really difficult bit was just beginning.

First, they needed a director. Macdonald originally hoped to use his brother Kevin, but Channel 4 wanted someone with more experience. After sending the script to 20 directors, Macdonald chose Danny Boyle—a director who had never made a feature film.

Born in Bolton, Lancashire in 1956, Boyle was a director with a growing reputation. He had made his name with the Royal Shakespeare Company, before becoming deputy director at the Royal Court between 1985 and 1987. In the late eighties he became bored with theatre, and left for television. He made films for the BBC in Northern Ireland, where he produced Alan Clark's controversial *Elephant*, and more recently he had directed the BBC series, *Mr Wroe's Virgins*, and two episodes of *Inspector Morse*.

Shallow Grave had been turned down by a number of directors who thought it was cold and heartless, but Boyle seized the opportunity with both hands. "When I read it I thought it was a really exciting script—clean and mean and truly cinematic in the way the Billy Wilder films are. I thought, I've got to do this. When I went for the audition I said it reminded me of *Blood Simple*, in its commitment to narrative and plot, which got me off on the right foot.

"Andrew didn't want someone like a Stephen Frears or Terry Gilliam, who was going to take over the script."

Boyle had said exactly what Macdonald wanted to hear, and the producer was delighted to give him the job. Having worked on films like *Revolution*, Macdonald had seen at first hand how poor planning could wreak havoc with a film's budget. On a £1 million movie like *Shallow Grave*, there was simply no room for mistakes, and he needed a director he could rely on completely.

Macdonald believed in a collaborative approach to making films—much like his grandfather before him—and this was an approach that suited Boyle. "Before I produced *Shallow Grave* I worked on several low-budget films as part of the production crew," Macdonald said afterwards. "I saw that an incredible amount of time and energy is wasted just trying to communicate what you want from other members of the crew. It always seemed that no-one could agree on what film they were trying to make. Everyone was trying to make their film—not *the* film. This always led to compromises, and ultimately to disaster; when you make a film for a million pounds there is no turning back. Once you start shooting, you cannot afford to reshoot unless the negative comes back black."

Macdonald wanted *Shallow Grave* to be a genuine collaboration—not only between his Figment Films team of Boyle and Hodge, but the principal cast, crew, financiers and distributors. "We all agreed that the script was the bible and . . . we would not waver from it," he said.

Boyle liked the way Macdonald worked, and was equally detailed in his preparation. He made up a scrapbook containing a series of images to give the others an idea of what he was trying to shoot, and also brought in people he had worked with before, including cinematographer Brian Tufano and film editor Masahiro Hirakubo, with whom he had made *Mr Wroe's Virgins*. New Zealand actress Kerry Fox, whom he knew from the same series, was also recruited to play one of the three main characters.

Robert Carlyle, regarded by many as one of the best British actors of his generation, auditioned for the part of wise-cracking journalist Alex Law. But it was Ewan McGregor who finally won the part. Boyle did not know McGregor, but the producer of *Mr Wroe's Virgins*, Ros Wolfes, had raved about him when Boyle phoned to find out what he was like in *Scarlet and Black*. When McGregor later met Boyle, Macdonald and Hodge, they took virtually no time to decide he was right for the part.

In September 1993, filming finally began. McGregor

travelled north from London for an intensive shoot that would last just 30 days, during which he shared a flat with Boyle, and fellow actors Kerry Fox and Christopher Eccleston, in an attempt to inject extra realism into their screen performances.

As Fox commented later: "We stayed in a flat to get to know one another. We did become quite close. In the film the three of us interview a string of prospective flatmates and are very rude to them. In the real flat we had a TV crew filming a documentary about the making of *Shallow Grave* and we found ourselves behaving in a very unpleasant manner towards them. I'm quite ashamed now, but the process did help us develop the characters. I even noticed Christopher becoming a bit reclusive, like he does in the movie."

Much of the film's budget was spent converting an old warehouse in Glasgow into a mock-up of the interior of an elegant New Town flat in Edinburgh where most of the film would be set. As a result, the wages of all involved were minimal—Macdonald, Boyle and Hodge were taking equal shares of £25,000, and the cast even less.

Macdonald set himself up in an office next to the warehouse where 20 days of the shoot took place. And they were long days, often lasting more than 12 hours. Every night Boyle and Macdonald would spend an extra few hours discussing their work, and viewing the rushes. Hodge was working as a locum at a hospital in Romford, near London, but still managed to get to the set to play a cameo role as a detective. McGregor's mum Carol also appeared on screen for a split-second at the beginning of the film as a prospective flatmate. Later, when she joined her son for the first cast and crew screening, she suddenly piped up: "Ooh, it's me. It's me." "It was brilliant," said Ewan. "She'd forgotten she was in it."

Behind the scenes, however, tempers sometimes frayed, and nerves were often strained to breaking point. In the TV documentary on the making of *Shallow Grave*, directed by Kevin Macdonald, the pressure on his older brother becomes clear as the shoot progresses. In one particularly embarrassing scene the producer discovers that 18 rolls of film, instead of 18 boxes, have been budgeted for. Suddenly he realises that there isn't enough film left to finish the movie.

"Don't be ridiculous," said Boyle.

"No, we're running out of film, we're not going to have any left," said Macdonald.

A crisis meeting had to be hastily organised to raise the money for more film. On another occasion, they planned to hire a million pounds for the day, complete with security guards. But in the end they could not afford to do it, and settled for fake cash instead.

Despite these difficulties, the film was completed on schedule, and overall it had been a tremendously successful shoot. As Boyle and Macdonald headed off to post-production, McGregor flew back to London unaware just how well the movie would turn out.

Boyle and Macdonald had always known the type of film they did not want to make—the kind of drab, depressing drama that starts out with a slow pan over the rooftops of a grey British city in the rain. Their film was going to be nothing like that. Instead, they wanted to create something in the style of a low-budget, off-the-wall American movie. They set out to make *Shallow Grave* dynamic and vibrant, shocking and entertaining, and were pretty confident that this was exactly what they had done.

By April 1994 the film was ready. The breathtaking fast-forward dash through Edinburgh's Georgian New Town backed by the dance music of Leftfield set the tone for an altogether different style of British movie. Boyle, Macdonald and Hodge modestly predicted they had made a decent B-movie, but even they could not have expected the astonishing response. At the Cannes Film Festival the following month, the reaction within the film-making community was sensational. Three extra screenings of *Shallow Grave* had to be arranged to meet the unprecedented demand to see it. At subsequent film festivals the response was equally positive, and by the time it went on general release in Britain the following January, *Shallow Grave* was the most eagerly awaited film since *Four Weddings and a Funeral*.

Boyle, Macdonald and Hodge were suddenly being hailed as the new heroes of British cinema. And Ewan McGregor was being celebrated as one of its finest young acting talents.

Meanwhile, McGregor's personal life was entering a period of dramatic change—he was about to get married.

X

ALL ABOUT EVE

Early in 1994, the word on *Shallow Grave* was already beginning to spread, even though Danny Boyle and Andrew
Macdonald were still at work editing the film. Ewan
McGregor, meanwhile, was back in London. The recent
success of *Scarlet and Black* had propelled his face—and
body—into the limelight. Shopping was no longer an entirely
private experience.

But he was also single again. His relationship with Marie
Pairis had come to an end, and they had decided to go their
separate ways. In September that year, on the *Shallow Grave*
set, he had become decidedly less willing to talk publicly
about his private life. In the *Sunday Mail*, interviewer Gavin

Docherty noted how he "clammed up like a venus flytrap" on the subject of real-life romance. "I have no time for women at the moment," he told Docherty. "There's nothing on the cards, and I'm quite happy about that."

Since the split with Marie, he had met other women, but shorter relationships no longer provided the excitement they once did. This was a far cry from the time, almost two years earlier, when McGregor moved into his bachelor pad in Primrose Hill. At that point, the last thing on his mind was long-term relationships. "The things that went on there . . ." he told one interviewer.

But early in 1994, he began to feel that the carefree lifestyle he had enjoyed for the majority of his time in London was no longer giving him the same kick. "I wasn't satisfied with it any more." He was beginning to feel that something was missing from his life. Sadly for his growing army of female fans, the time when their idol was single and available was about to come to an end. McGregor didn't know it then, but he was just weeks away from falling in love with another Frenchwoman—Eve Mavrakis.

The couple met on the set of the first episode of the ITV series, *Kavanagh QC*. Eve was an assistant to the art director, whilst McGregor was playing a rapist in the gripping story that was scheduled to launch John Thaw's latest TV series. Like Marie Pairis, Eve was a very attractive brunette. Asked later why he liked French women, McGregor answered, with a smile: "They're difficult. I like difficult women."

Eve Mavrakis was born on June 22, 1966 in the Dordogne

region of France. She was the older of two children and her parents, like McGregor's, worked in the education system— as college lecturers. But Eve's childhood did not mirror the comfortable, stable upbringing enjoyed by Ewan in Crieff. Her parents, Constantin and Annie Joelle, divorced when she was just five. Annie remarried a few years later, and it was not long before her new husband's work commitments required him to move halfway across the world to China. Annie and her two girls—aged just nine and four—went with him. For a young girl, moving to such an alien culture could have proved a harrowing and traumatic experience, but Eve embraced it. The strange environment helped form a personality that would forever be keen to explore new things and take on new challenges. In China she adapted well, maturing quickly beyond her years, providing invaluable support for her mother, who struggled with the new way of life. Eve's younger sister Marianne remembered how quickly Eve picked up Mandarin, showing a marvellous aptitude which would later see her fluent in four languages. She acted almost as a translator for her mother, who found it more difficult to adapt. "My sister has a great facility for languages," said Marianne. "She spoke Chinese as a child and was a great help to my mother, being able to translate things back into French."

The family returned to France a few years later, where Eve excelled in school, and was described as "confident, outgoing and intelligent." Marianne also recalled how Eve helped her mother look after their stepbrother Raphaelle, who was born when she was in high school. "When Eve was young she took on a lot of responsibility," said Marianne. "She looked after me a lot, and then when Raphaelle arrived she was like a mother to him. The link between Eve, myself and our brother is a strong one. If there are any problems we know we can count on each other. Eve is always very responsible."

Like McGregor with Hannah Titley, Eve got involved in her first big relationship at 17 with a local boy named Thierry. It lasted for two years before the couple split up, and the mature teenager, who studied French cinema at college, specialising in set design, returned once more to the Far East. She tried her hand at radio journalism and worked on TV and film projects, using her linguistic abilities to the full as a translator on Steven Spielberg's *Empire of the Sun*. Eve also learned to write in Chinese characters, a difficult skill few Westerners master.

Confident and mature, Eve came to London in the early 1990s, a city she grew to like better than Paris because of its more diverse, cosmopolitan feel. Fluent in French, English, Mandarin and Spanish, she could handle a number of different production jobs on a film set. In London she worked on TV adverts, shows and films, including the highly acclaimed *Bandit Queen*, the thriller *The Innocent Sleep*, and *Limited Edition*. She dressed better than the often scruffy McGregor, and took a keen interest in fashion. A lover of modern art and cinema, Eve was also a compulsive reader. "It's very important Eve has an interest and is discovering new things about life," said Marianne. "She always wants to be doing something constructive and interesting with every day and she is very independent."

McGregor was bowled over when he first met the cultured Mavrakis. "I knew from the first day I saw her," he said. "She's beautiful, so beautiful. The second I saw her I thought if I could be with her it would be like nothing I've ever had before. And I completely believe I will be with her forever, that we'll go through everything together."

It was while playing the rapist on *Kavanagh QC* that McGregor inspired similar feelings in Eve Mavrakis. First, Eve phoned her mother with the news she had fallen head over heels in love, and then she told Marianne. "She told me he was an actor, that he lived in London and that he wasn't famous. She said it was just the start of his career but that she was so proud and happy. When she met Ewan she felt very, very strongly that he was the man for her. She knew deep down he was the love of her life. When Eve was in England she had a few English boyfriends, but she is not a girl who sleeps around. As soon as she met Ewan she knew he was Mr Right."

As in McGregor's previous serious relationships, the couple grew very close quickly, and the bachelor pad soon took on a whole new look when Eve moved in. A few months later they decided to get married. "They see life in the same way," said Marianne.

The wedding took place in July 1995 in the tiny village of Festalemps in the Dordogne. Eve borrowed a spacious, secluded house with a large garden and a huge swimming pool, and sixty friends and family arrived for a week of relaxed celebration.

The ceremony itself, conducted in the local town hall by the mayor, M Debet, was a simple one, if slightly bizarre. McGregor was not looking his best. He had just finished shooting *Trainspotting*, in which he played the emaciated heroin addict Mark Renton. For the role he had lost more than two stones, and had a skinhead haircut. Dressed in a light-coloured suit, his hair had grown only a few millimetres by the time he and Eve tied the knot in the tiny French village. She, on the other hand, looked radiant in a simple, sleeveless dress.

The exchanging of vows was a strange experience for McGregor. Everything was said in French, so he had virtually no idea what was going on. After a little coaching, he made his only contribution to the ceremony. "All I said was 'Oui' and I'm not sure I said that at the right time," he joked.

Their subsequent wedding banquet was a delightful affair, with a typically nervous groom. "It was a wonderful wedding, just the way they wanted," said Jim McGregor, who flew out to France with Carol, and a number of the clan. "But he was the most nervous person I have ever seen when he was doing his speech."

When Ewan sat down, he breathed a sigh of relief before sitting up straight. He turned to his father: "Dad, I completely forgot to mention Eve."

"So I told him to stand up and give her a mention," said Jim later. "It was extremely funny."

For the rest of the week, the atmosphere was relaxed as the assorted friends and family members cooked local delicacies and sipped wine long into the night. It was exactly how Ewan had hoped it would be. "We all cooked for each other at night, drank fine wines in the garden," he said. "You know how it can become completely out of your hands? Well, it was absolutely what we wanted to do. That's very unusual, when you have a dream, to actually see it totally realised, which our marriage was. It was perfect."

During the *Kavanagh QC* shoot Ewan and Eve's relationship was known to some, but not all—even the show's producer Chris Kelly only found out afterwards. "They were very discreet," he said. "She was petite, pretty, extremely charming and very good at her job."

Kelly did not fail, however, to recognise McGregor's ability and professionalism. Ewan was cast in the demanding role of university student David Armstrong, who is accused of forcing a bored housewife to have sex. This was the opening episode of the new ITV legal drama, starring John Thaw, who was loved by millions in his previous role as the eccentric Inspector Morse. Thaw was hoping to repeat that success in his new role as a Lancashire barrister.

As usual, McGregor made a particularly good impression during his audition. Afterwards, the show's casting director Joyce Gallie scored a large star in her diary next to his name. This was a rare occurrence—something she only did when she had witnessed a rare talent.

In this episode, *Nothing But The Truth*, McGregor's character,

Armstrong, takes a summer job working as a builder at the home of the middle-aged housewife played by Alison Steadman. She accuses him of rape, and Kavanagh is called in to defend him. Warming to the charming young student, and fully convinced of his innocence, Kavanagh succeeds in securing an acquittal. After the trial, however, the barrister is approached by a young woman who says she too was raped by Armstrong, and the episode concludes with a chilling shot of Armstrong holding a photograph of Kavanagh's teenage daughter.

Later, McGregor joked about the "romantic" circumstances in which he met Eve for the first time. "My future wife was sitting upstairs and I was raping Alison Steadman downstairs," he said. "She says she can remember sitting upstairs listening to us. It was fantastic."

Kelly was convinced he had worked with a major new talent. "He had to be this adorable young man which he played so convincingly. He still wasn't too well known when he worked on *Kavanagh*, and he was very excited to be working. He was very committed without wearing it on his sleeve."

On one occasion, as the production was threatening to overrun, McGregor and actress Geraldine James saved the day by doing a difficult ten-minute scene in one take. To get five minutes in the can in one day was considered exceptional. "They did this massively long scene because we had got into terrible time difficulties," recalled Kelly. "Ewan and Geraldine saved it by doing an 11-page scene in just one take. It was quite remarkable. I vividly remember travelling back to London with him by car, and I made it quite clear he was definitely going to be very big. He was very confident, but very modest too."

At this stage McGregor's earnings were also modest— nothing like the sort of figures normally associated with "stars". For his role in *Kavanagh QC*, he would have done well to pick up £8,000. For *Doggin' Around* and *Blue Juice*, two films he shot around the same time, the rewards would have been similarly limited.

Doggin' Around was a one-off BBC comedy drama, most notable for the rare appearance of Elliot Gould in a British TV production. He plays an ageing American jazz pianist, Joe Warren, who comes to England for the first time in 10 years to play at the famous Ronnie Scott's jazz club. Unfortunately for him, his original itinerary is replaced by a tour of small working-class clubs in the North of England. As the tour progresses, so his past, including huge debts, catches up with him.

McGregor plays one of the band who accompany Gould during his various skirmishes with audiences, criminals and the police. Although the film was well received, its screening in a late-night slot on a Sunday ensured modest ratings.

Blue Juice, McGregor's final project in 1994, was his biggest to date. At £2 million, the film's budget was double that of *Shallow Grave*. The money was being put up by Channel 4— the same people who had made *Shallow Grave* possible, and the cast included his friend Sean Pertwee.

According to Peter Salmi, the film's producer, McGregor was well enough known by that time to have pulled out of *Blue Juice* in favour of more lucrative roles. But as it turned out he was happy to be involved with a project that would at best only earn him around £20,000. Although McGregor was being offered more scripts than ever, he liked the sound of this one, and was keen to be part of a movie that was already being dubbed "*American Graffiti* on surfboards".

The word "surf" is generally associated with sun, sand and coral seas. But not on this occasion—*Blue Juice* may have been about surfers, but it was set in Cornwall on the south-west coast of England. Even more surprisingly, it would be filmed in October and November, two of the coldest months of the year—although some of Pertwee's on-board scenes were actually shot in the more hospitable waters of Lanzarote, off the west coast of Africa.

The movie's stars, McGregor, Pertwee, Steven Macintosh and Peter Gunn, had surfing lessons before filming began. "Ewan McGregor and I came down about a week before filming to just hang out and get a feel for the lifestyle," said Pertwee. "I was amazed by the intellect of these guys. When they talk about pollution at sea they know exactly what they're talking about. Surfing is very good for your soul, and I really mean that. It's like riding on fire. The mental feeling is extraordinary."

Unfortunately, the pollution laid McGregor low during filming. "I remember Ewan was under the weather a bit with a virus," said Salmi. "We think it was because of the sewage in the water, that there might have been some nasty bugs going around. A few people were affected." McGregor recuperated in a lodge owned by The Treganna Castle hotel in St Ives, where the four male leads were staying. According to Salmi, rather than being put off by the polluted sea and freezing conditions, the cast positively embraced the surfing scene for the two months they were there. "A couple of guys down there, Rob Jack and Steve England, were really into the whole scene," said Salmi, "and they showed us the way. Some days the boys would spend half the day on a board. I think that was one of the best bits, living the life down there. They are pretty hard-core guys."

In the film, McGregor plays drug dealer Dean Raymond, one of a trio of London-based friends who drop in on their surfing buddy played by Pertwee, whose relationship with his girlfriend, played by Catherine Zeta Jones, is beginning to fall apart. The arrival of McGregor, techno DJ Macintosh and pub landlord Gunn only makes things worse, but after a series of misadventures everyone involved lives happily ever after.

McGregor clearly enjoyed making *Blue Juice*: "I had a great time, filming in Cornwall for ten weeks. . . . I've never partied so much in my life." And his performance as the cocky, yet insecure Dean—who believes selling drugs to kids is a justifiable way of making a living—stands out, alongside that of Peter Gunn as the pub landlord who spends most of the film spaced out on Ecstasy. Their performances, however, were just about the only things that shone in this production.

Ewan himself recognised the movie's failings: "It's a bit muddled in the middle, it's just a shame, it's not really very good."

Blue Juice was the first feature film from director Carl Prechezer and producer Peter Salmi, and their inexperience showed. The film was a mess, poorly thought out and directed, and the climax where Pertwee saves McGregor from the raging waves verges on the ridiculous. "We bit off a little bit more than we could chew," admitted Salmi.

During McGregor's time in Cornwall, Eve was a frequent visitor. "When she came down they were very close," recalled Salmi. "You could see they were very serious." With marriage only eight months away, McGregor was enjoying a contented personal life, and as he left the set of *Blue Juice*, he was also excited about the prospects for *Shallow Grave. Four Weddings and a Funeral* was on its way to becoming the biggest grossing British movie of all time, and, as the British film industry experienced yet another of its periodic revivals, *Shallow Grave* could hardly have arrived at a better time. Originally destined for the art-house circuit, *Shallow Grave* would turn out to be the biggest British movie of the year.

XI

GRAVEDIGGING

Shallow Grave, as its title suggests, was dark and macabre. It had a brilliant script, and had been produced by some of the most promising young talent in the industry, but no-one could have predicted the impact it would have when Boyle finally finished editing in April 1994. Even Ewan McGregor was left awestruck when he first saw a rough cut, commenting: "God, did we really shoot this film?"

A few months earlier, Channel 4 executives had gone to France with roughs for the Cannes Film Festival's selection panel. Robert Jones, an independent buyer for Polygram, liked what he saw, and offered £2 million for the international distribution rights, including the all-important American market. The makers were delighted as this meant that, a year before its release, the film had more than paid for itself. For the next 12 months *Shallow Grave* was on the crest of a wave of critical approval at film festivals. Much to the delight of Hodge, comparisons were drawn with Tarantino's first big hit, *Reservoir Dogs*.

Shallow Grave kicks off speeding through the streets of Edinburgh's New Town, before three flatmates, played by McGregor, Kerry Fox and Christopher Eccleston, mercilessly humiliate a series of applicants for the spare bedroom in their elegant top-floor flat. Eventually, the mysterious novelist Hugo, played by Keith Allen, gets the room. Unfortunately, he dies almost immediately from a heroin overdose, and when the curious flatmates finally break his door down, they discover a stark naked Hugo dead on the bed, and a suitcase full of money underneath it.

The dilemma for journalist Alex Law (McGregor), doctor Juliet Miller (Fox) and accountant David Stephens (Eccleston), is what to do with the cash—and the corpse. They decide to keep the money, and dispose of the body—a decision which leads them to a wood at dead of night, where the corpse is gruesomely dismembered before being buried in a shallow grave. At this point everything goes disastrously wrong, and their lives begin to fall apart. Hugo's extremely violent criminal associates turn up looking for the cash, the police start asking questions, and the once-friendly flatmates, now greedy and cynical, betray each other. Macdonald affectionately called it a story of "love, trust, friendship . . . sex, violence, evil, greed, anger, betrayal, death, dismemberment, and disposal."

"I liked this from the start, because it had a great script and they knew what they were doing," said David Aukin, Channel 4's head of drama, who gave the go-ahead to fund the film. "But you never know which ones are going to be a hit." Although McGregor as the cynical journalist and Eccleston as the increasingly unhinged accountant produced the strongest acting performances, the real revelation in *Shallow Grave* was Boyle's direction. His interpretation of Hodge's script, handling the twists and turns of plot with confidence and verve, turned what could have been a fairly routine thriller into an unforgettable cinematic experience.

Boyle also made particularly good use of the limited budget. Most of the action takes place within the Georgian flat set, but thanks to stylish direction and design this never seems restrictive, simply adding to the film's dark and increasingly claustrophobic atmosphere, as the former friends turn against each other within these familiar sur-roundings.

The official world premiere of *Shallow Grave* took place at the 1994 Edinburgh Film Festival, where local critics were surprisingly lukewarm—one even described it as a load of old garbage.

But these reviewers were sadly out of step with the reaction everywhere else. The following year *Shallow Grave* played to sell-out audiences in Britain for weeks, became the most profitable British film of the year, and finally raked in more than £20 million worldwide. Known in some non-English-speaking countries under the title *Little Murders Between Friends*, it picked up awards in France, Spain, Portugal, Italy and at Robert Redford's influential Sundance Festival in Utah. It also won BAFTA's Alexander Korda award for the year's outstanding British film. The critics were more or less united: *Variety* described it as a "tar-black comedy that zings along on a wave of visual and scripting inventiveness . . . pure movie-making." "Hitchcock would have admired its ruthlessness and cruel humour," summed up *The Observer's* Philip French.

Macdonald, who was becoming known as one of the most shrewd and talented producers in the business, was nothing less than delighted: "I think the film looks like an $8 million movie, not a £1 million movie," he said. "It is being shown a lot in Hollywood and they are going wild about it over there . . . and coming up with all sorts of ridiculous offers."

For Ewan McGregor, *Shallow Grave* was a turning-point in an already successful career. His performance as Alex Law was generally well received—although not by the *Glasgow Herald's* film critic, William Russell, who called him "pretty, but pretty unconvincing." But in the wake of the film's success came intense media interest in its rising young star. It was to be McGregor's first real experience of facing the hype head-on. Promoting the movie at a festival in France, he was astonished at some of the questions posed by reporters—one even asked his opinion on whether the film was a backlash against naked capitalism in the western world.

"They seem to analyse things more than we do and seek out the moral messages," McGregor said later. "The interviewers really put you on the spot in terms of your understanding of the film. Sometimes it just becomes too much. I feel like saying: 'I just learned the lines. Ask Danny or John.'"

At this point, Boyle, Hodge and Macdonald were revelling in the acclaim the film had brought them. They told everyone the secret of their success was working as a team—and the fact that they actually liked each other. Their approach to making movies heralded the arrival of a new order in British film-making that did not limit itself to cosy period dramas or bleak, depressing modern realism. They had opened the door for a new generation of movie-makers.

"We never expected it to have the kind of success it has had," remarked Boyle in the aftermath. "It was an attempt to make an invigorating and exciting low-budget British film, which meant the narrative became the principal ingredient. The narrative was our god."

Their style was clearly influenced by the work of the American independents, although Boyle often said the trio had no specific agenda, but were interested in telling things as they really were. Explaining this approach, he drew parallels with Pulp's album *Different Class*. "A lot of the album is about Jarvis Cocker's experiences," he said, "and you realise that's what art is really, just trying to write about your experiences as they happen." Macdonald suggested their achievement mirrored that of groups like Blur, Oasis and Pulp. "They're writing pop songs instead of great screenplays," he said.

Rejecting criticism that the film was unconvincing in its development of the characters, Boyle argued: "I've spent a lot of my career building up plausible characters, which intellectuals find rewarding and interesting, but the public doesn't give a fuck. They have a slightly different agenda. Now you can either despise them for their lack of rigour, or you can in some way embrace them and give them, in terms of a British film, some slightly different things. That is what we were trying to do."

"We're not up on a hill waiting for the masses to arrive," said Macdonald. "What's important are those who actually commit their five pounds a week to the cinema. Our films may prove worthless in ten year's time, so we've set ourselves up to engage with that audience now rather than let it come to us." Hodge was equally forthright. "We're not making films for the critics in London, we're making them for the people who pay and queue up on a Friday night. The commercial imperative, having to survive in the marketplace, I think makes good films."

Hollywood soon came knocking on their doors, but a departure across the Atlantic was far from a foregone conclusion. Boyle was offered the chance to direct Sharon Stone. "We've been taken out to lunch by Disney, by Fox—we've had some crazy offers," said Macdonald. Hodge was deluged with agents wanting to read his scripts—he was even asked to come up with something for Gene Hackman. One mogul offered the trio £250,000 to do whatever project they wanted.

But Hollywood was to be disappointed—for now at least.

"What I want to do is stay working with Andrew and John," said Boyle. "What we do is very much the product of three film-makers."

The trio worked as a team, and wanted to retain control of their work. Which was something the power brokers of Hollywood were reluctant to concede. Macdonald wanted to stay in Britain where they could use the momentum built up by *Shallow Grave*. "Hollywood wants to control individuals, hoping that what it likes about them will rub off on their product," he added. "It's a deal with the devil, and that's why it's for millions." Instead of taking the money and catching the next plane to LA, Boyle, Macdonald and Hodge were determined to stay together for a more ambitious and risky project.

The idea for his next film first came to Macdonald just after the *Shallow Grave* shoot ended in December, 1993. He was on a flight home to Scotland reading a novel he had been given by a friend. It was *Trainspotting* by Irvine Welsh.

In Scotland, where the book is set, it had achieved cult status. Although on the surface the subject was bleak and depressing, Welsh's riotous and highly original trip through the highs and horrors of the heroin underclass of 1980s Edinburgh was gripping stuff. His writing style was unique, filled with the kind of vibrancy, energy and expletives to which no literary tradition could relate. While many people loathed the book, an even greater number loved its celebration of an extraordinary subculture. Welsh's bold, brash, curiously parochial approach (much of the dialogue is written in local dialect) hit a raw nerve and *Trainspotting* quickly became a huge bestseller.

Macdonald read the book with increasing interest. He noted some obvious points—it had no clear plot; it was a fragmented, episodic collection of short stories; it was written in language few people outside Edinburgh would understand; it was packed full of expletives; and, most controversially, it portrayed the positive aspects of the heroin addict's lifestyle in unprecedented detail. Most British film-makers would have steered well clear of such potentially explosive subject matter—but Macdonald did not hesitate: he knew it would make a great movie.

He set about persuading Boyle, who thought the book was brilliant but pointed out there was "fuck all" of a story. This, he thought, could be a problem, but Macdonald was undeterred. Dr Hodge's magic typewriter would surely do the trick.

"The idea right from the beginning was to work out a way of doing it that was as amazing in film terms as the book was in book terms," said Macdonald. "I had no idea how to tell the story or even what the story was. Danny felt the same way. John gave his copy of the book to someone else. I knew he liked it, but to convince him to write it into a screenplay was quite a tall order."

Hodge told the others that *Trainspotting* was amazing, but would never make a film. Macdonald and Boyle, however, were persistent. They refused to take no for an answer.

For almost a year they discussed which bits of the novel

could be incorporated into the film. Hodge doubted whether he could produce a script that would do justice to the complexity and diversity of the text. He had to find a way to make a film about drug abuse appealing to cinema-goers. Eventually, by November 1994, Hodge had hammered out 50 pages of a first draft. Over Christmas, he completed a more detailed revised draft which was sent out to prospective backers.

In Hodge's screenplay some of Welsh's original characters were dropped, others were amalgamated, and some minor details became the inspiration for major scenes. He missed out his favourite chapter, "Memories of Matty", which he felt would have made a cracking film on its own. "You've got to be ruthless," Hodge said. "You've just got to say, 'we're not making a tribute to the book, we're trying to make a film.'" "If you're going to compare us to the book," said Boyle, "we have to hold our hands up and say, 'you're right, the book is better, it is a masterpiece, it is ten films in one.'" Hodge also decided Mark Renton, the book's most entertaining character, would become the focus of the movie. The story would unfold around his life, the highs and lows of his entanglement in drugs, climaxing in the betrayal of his former friends in order to escape from the heroin underworld. "One of the great things about the book," said Hodge, "is that amidst all these horrific circumstances this character is still alive and kicking. He's still got a smart comment to make and he's still got a heart—maybe a slightly damaged and bitter one, but he's still a human being and so are the people around him."

Unsurprisingly, potential backers were initially deeply

sceptical about the project. Tales of drug abuse were generally regarded as poison at the box office. But Boyle, Macdonald and Hodge were hot property at that moment, and soon the offers started to roll in.

While they were promoting *Shallow Grave* at Robert Redford's Sundance Film Festival in Utah, Channel 4 agreed to provide the £1.5 million budget for *Trainspotting*. Polygram International took on the marketing and distribution. Hollywood studios had offered more money, but control over the finished product was more important than cash, and Channel 4 would allow them the freedom they required. "We were the only people who could get *Trainspotting* made," said Macdonald. "We had just had an international success and could do anything we wanted. I know it sounds arrogant, but we had the clout to convince the industry to trust us with the money to film a book with heroin and dead babies in it."

Remarkably, all this was agreed before the trio secured the film rights to the book, and it was not until March 1995, just two months before the shoot was due to start, that a contract was signed.

For Ewan McGregor, there was no casting session. As far as Macdonald and Boyle were concerned, the role of Renton was made for him, and they gave him a copy of the script at the Sundance festival in America. Even so, at that point they were just asking him to look at it. "Those bastards," said McGregor. "They gave me the script on the understanding there was no presumption that I would be in the film. I read it and thought: 'I've got to play this part.'"

Initially, Hodge had doubts about McGregor as Renton. "I only found this out recently, but he didn't think I was the right guy for the job at all. The other two had to convince him. Hopefully he feels differently now."

Boyle and Macdonald were adamant: "Ewan was a logical choice," said Boyle. "Ewan has phenomenal technical skill which allows him to use the camera to its full extent. He's actually not the most gorgeous looking person—he's not one of the drop dead gorgeous Brad Pitt types—but there's something about him that's attractive because he's more human. He has that slight edge of the boy-next-door."

Hodge finally agreed. Later McGregor described getting the role as like receiving "a million birthday presents". Jonny Lee Miller as Sick Boy, Ewen Bremner as Spud, Kevin McKidd as Tommy and Kelly Macdonald as Diane were soon on board. Perhaps the biggest coup was persuading Robert Carlyle to accept the role of Begbie. *Shallow Grave*'s Christopher Eccleston had been considered, but the trio finally chose Carlyle. At that point in his career he could have justifiably refused to do a part with a lower billing than McGregor, but he later reflected on his decision to accept the role as one of the best he ever made.

Everything was now ready for the making of *Trainspotting*. It would be the most profitable film in the world in 1996, and it would make Ewan McGregor an international star.

XII

TRAINSPOTTING

The old Wills cigarette factory was baking under a hot Glasgow sun. Irvine Welsh stood outside, squinting against the light, then retreated into the shade. Inside, the cool, cavernous interior was a hive of activity, unaffected by the unusually warm weather. All around him people rushed about, engaged in a multiplicity of unknown tasks. Welsh was on the set of *Trainspotting*, preparing for his cameo role as shady drug dealer Mikey Forrester. Many of the locations used in the movie were in the old Wills factory, as were the production offices, where Andrew Macdonald appeared to spend every waking moment.

Welsh surveyed the scene before him. When he had written

the book he had never imagined it would be published. Now they were making *Trainspotting* into a film, and he was in it. "There's aw these punters runnin' aroond like blue-arsed flies, aw this organisation and aw this money being spent," Welsh told one interviewer. "Just 'cos I sat down three years ago and started typing."

But behind the frenetic activity of the film set lay months of careful preparation. For Ewan McGregor the preparation had been particularly rigorous. If he was going to look convincing as a junkie, he would have to lose weight. To become Mark Renton he needed to shed two stones to be exact—and quick.

McGregor immediately cut beer, milk and butter from his diet. Eve cooked special meals, forcing him to toe the line.

"Ewan is normally quite a chunky guy," said Boyle. "But he fucked off, and six weeks later he walked in and he was like a stick."

McGregor looked dreadful. His head had been shaved, his cheekbones had begun to protrude, and his eyes were shadowed—but, more importantly, he looked the part. "I felt really good that way, really agile and nice."

Losing weight was not a problem. "That was just something that had to be done," he said. "Renton was living a life on heroin, so he wasn't going to be a beefcake. There was almost nothing difficult about the film because I was so prepared for it. I had such a passion for it before we started, and that stayed with me right through the shoot."

The actor approached the challenge of *Trainspotting* with

gusto. He had started his diet a few months earlier when filming Peter Greenaway's erotic odyssey, *The Pillow Book*. He told friends to watch that film closely. They would notice how his character was noticeably thinner at the end of the movie than the beginning.

The shadow of heroin had descended on Edinburgh at roughly the same time Ewan McGregor was starting school 50 miles away in Crieff. Whilst Irvine Welsh was observing the grim events unfolding in the capital, McGregor was blissfully unaware of it. He once said he never tried drugs for fear of upsetting his parents. "We didn't really do any drugs because there weren't any to be had," he said. "I missed the whole rave scene and the E culture in the late eighties. It's quite sad. They really got the wrong guy for the job. Ewan 'Mr Nae Drugs' McGregor."

Soon the image of McGregor as the soaking, emaciated skinhead would appear on billboards all over Britain. The haunting visage of Mark Renton would become an enduring image not only for the film, but for the drugs culture that had inspired it.

For other members of the cast the world of *Trainspotting* was closer to home, as Ewen Bremner, who played Spud, knew only too well: "I felt these characters were part of my heritage. I'm from Portobello, which is only a couple of miles from Leith, where *Trainspotting* is set. I grew up surrounded by that world." Robert Carlyle expressed similar sentiments, but for Ewan McGregor the culture was largely alien.

After McGregor was offered the part, he read Welsh's

book for the first time. He knew it was imperative to try and get inside the psyche of the anti-heroic Renton, a character addicted to the highs of shooting up, yet intelligent enough to realise its futility. McGregor then read every book he could find on drug abuse, and when he was completing *The Pillow Book* in Luxembourg, even observed a group of junkies at a railway station, noting their spaced-out mannerisms. "I just watched them from a distance, I'd never initiate myself into the group because that would be too embarrassing," he said, adding in a mock actor's voice: "Hi, I'm going to play a drug addict. Would you like to show me how to do it?"

On his return to Scotland, the crew and some of the cast talked to real-life addicts in Leith, where the book is set. It was a depressing experience, and put doubts in Boyle's mind about his ability to make an entertaining film from such grim subject matter. Those fears were allayed when they met members of Calton Athletic, a drugs rehabilitation unit in Glasgow that helped junkies back on to the straight and narrow. "These guys are fanatical," said Boyle. "It was inspirational to see these ordinary people with no money or job prospects, struggling to give up this creature that has taken them over."

The *Trainspotting* team played football with the Calton team, and were usually well beaten. McGregor and the others also sat in on sessions where the former addicts relayed their horrific experiences. They winced at stories of people dying and being left to rot under their beds, of mothers forgetting they had given birth, of successful lives going down the tubes because of one initial hit. "I'd never heard anything like it," said McGregor. "I'd never felt anything like the atmosphere of support in the room; the giving of strength to each other, from these hard men and women, felt almost religious."

"To meet them," said Boyle, "you get that feeling of seeing life again in people who have been away from us. They came along and showed us everything. Anything in the book, they've done much, much worse."

Calton's project leader was Eamon Doherty. He started taking drugs at 13, was injecting heroin twice a week within two years, and had the last rites read by a priest when he was admitted to hospital aged 17 suffering from hepatitis, arthritis and blood poisoning. He recovered, continuing as before, but in 1991 gave up heroin because "the hit had gone".

Doherty became the official adviser on *Trainspotting*. McGregor's portrayal of "cold turkey" was so convincing because Doherty knew the feeling only too well. And Doherty ensured the graphic scene where Renton cooks up was utterly realistic, and shocking. He coached each of the cast over and over again on how to do it properly. "He came round and he marked us all on it," said Kevin McKidd. "It was just like Bruce Forsyth's *Generation Game*. By the end it had become second nature." McGregor also became used to a never-ending supply of needles sticking in his arm. "It is my arm," he said, referring to the gruesome scenes in the film, "but moulded prosthetically and with a plastic pipe going into a little pool of blood underneath, so you can see the pulse."

The seven-week shoot started in May 1995, after two weeks of rehearsals in a Glasgow tower block. Kelly Macdonald had just landed the role of schoolgirl Diane, after being selected from hundreds of unknowns who responded to flyers handed out in Glasgow's pubs, clubs and hairdressers. One of her first tasks as an actress was to strip off for a love scene with McGregor. They had rehearsed the scene fully dressed, but Macdonald became nervous when she saw the double bed.

"I don't want to do it," she said. Boyle looked at her, smiled and said: "Just get under the covers and pretend you're doing a radio play. Just make the sounds."

From Glasgow, the crew went to London for a few days filming, then into editing for eight weeks. The film they finally produced zooms along at lightning pace. It is brilliant, horrible, and achingly sad. It is both ninety minutes of pure entertainment, and a chilling vision of the lowest, most vile and aimless existence imaginable. It tells the story of Mark Renton and his mates—Spud, Sick Boy, Tommy and Begbie— a bunch of losers whose world revolves around the pursuit and consumption of heroin. In one of the most memorable scenes Renton dives down the "worst toilet in Scotland" to recover opium suppositories. In another a baby dies, its mother too "scoobied" to notice, while the only relatively clean-living character dies of AIDS, and the extreme violence of the psychopathic Begbie is an accepted part of everyday life. As their world falls apart, Renton is the only one who manages to "choose life", escaping with the proceeds of a drugs deal to make a new start.

The film's success, however, would be due to the team's refusal to depict these events in a depressingly realistic style. They wanted to create an entertaining adaptation of Welsh's work, not a documentary. The surreal toilet scene is a typical example, ending with Renton swimming underwater in a blue lagoon to Brian Eno's *Deep Blue Day*. "The book is very clear about what it would be like to put your arm down among strangers' excrement," said Macdonald. "Symbolically, the chapter is about how far you are prepared to go for your heroin, and that's what it's about in the film. Besides, if you did it absolutely realistically it would be unwatchable."

Trainspotting's promotion went into overdrive before the world premiere in Glasgow, and the official British release in London and Scotland on February 23. From March, people all over the UK were desperate to see it. Initially, Polygram intended to aim *Trainspotting* mainly at the youth market, but after seeing the final cut, they decided it would be suitable for a wider audience. Around £150,000 would normally be spent promoting a movie made for £1.5 million, but for *Trainspotting*, the figure was £800,000. A soundtrack featuring Pulp, Primal Scream, Underworld, Leftfield, Iggy Pop and Lou Reed, and day-glo orange posters featuring McGregor, Carlyle, Macdonald, Miller and Bremner in their now instantly recognisable poses, propelled the film into the nation's consciousness long before its release.

Then the long-expected controversy over the depiction of heroin abuse blew up. Mark Renton's memorable "Choose Life" summary of the joys of shooting up sparked off a storm of protest. Dealing with taboo subject matter in such a manner was too much for some, and the *Trainspotting* team were accused of glamorising heroin. Anti-drugs groups said it would lead to more youngsters trying the drug. The *Daily Mail* was scathing: "[It] is a disgusting little film—even more disgusting than it knows." One of the paper's columnists, Christopher Tookey, commented: "*Trainspotting* pours scorn on conventional values and pokes fun at capitalism while subscribing to a much more vicious and depressingly consumerist ethos of its own. It is not a film I would care to have on my conscience." In the *Evening Standard*, Alexander Walker said: "In style, structure and subversive imagination it recalls Stanley Kubrick's *A Clockwork Orange*. . . . Kubrick's film made one think. Boyle's film, overall a clever pastiche of the senior director's style, makes one puke." In America, one newspaper said it made *Kids* look like *Sesame Street*. Even the Republican presidential candidate, Bob Dole, mentioned the film in an attack on Hollywood's portrayal of drug abuse. Another British newspaper columnist, George Birrell, was equally vitriolic. *Trainspotting*, he wrote, was "juvenile, inane, puerile". He described the infamous toilet scene as having been "very realistically filmed"—a remarkable statement—before concluding: "If this film does not bomb in America then my name's Martin Scorsese."

Inevitably, McGregor became the focus for much of the

flak. There was even speculation he had tried heroin to prepare for the role of Renton. McGregor admitted he approached the part feeling that there was a certain glamour attached to the subject of heroin, but this view was soundly thrashed out of him after two weeks listening to the experiences of the former addicts in Glasgow. "Hearing how low these hard men and women had sunk certainly dispelled the idea," he said. "Any mystique I had before about heroin is completely gone now. I'm not as judgmental about addicts as I used to be. I know more about their suffering, their pain and their need for help."

On another occasion, he said: "I thought about actually taking heroin and the more research I did, the less I wanted to do it. I didn't think it was necessary. I've had to die on screen before, and I don't know what that's like either. To take heroin for the part would be just an excuse to take heroin. So I didn't."

Amid all the furore, the *Trainspotting* team resolutely defended their product. "All the traditional information about heroin is there," said Boyle. "It's just used in a form that is going to get people into the cinema rather than repel them. We wanted to be honest about heroin, so the beginning of *Trainspotting* is highly seductive. The dilemma was that we wanted to make an entertaining film about something that is potentially lethal, and this is something that people may find unacceptable.

"In the end it conforms to every other film about heroin. It shows you how it will destroy you. But there are people . . .

who go through it and come out the other side. You've got to tell the truth about that, even though you are accused of encouraging drug use."

"Some people will have you believe that it must be unpleasant and will destroy your life," said Hodge, who as a doctor in Edinburgh saw at first-hand the consequences of drug abuse. "But I think the truth is closer to the fact that it is pleasant and will destroy your life."

McGregor was equally forthright. "Five people shooting up heroin is a lot less extreme than blowing someone's face off with a gun, which people are happy to watch. That's mainstream."

On another occasion, he said: "This is the way it is. It's there for your own interpretation. Heroin is obviously not a good thing, as you can see from what happens to several characters in the film. But, also we're not saying these characters are evil bastards, that only evil bastards do drugs. I don't think this film will promote heroin use at all. Unless people are very stupid." In a later interview, clearly angry at the constant questioning, he said: "I'm sick to death of people saying *Trainspotting* glamorised heroin. I mean, were these idiots watching? It didn't, it's as simple as that."

The people who criticised the film were a vociferous minority. The vast majority loved *Trainspotting*. *Empire* magazine called it the movie of the decade, whilst other magazines said it was the most exciting film about British youth since *Quadrophenia*.

Undeniably, *Trainspotting* was hip. It was set in the early eighties but was backed by a nineties soundtrack. Boyle said the film, through its depiction of the heroin underclass of the eighties, was speaking to the Ecstasy generation of the nineties.

Merely putting something on screen almost inevitably gives it a degree of glamour. Making it highly entertaining and side-splittingly funny simply reinforces the effect.

"It does worry me that the characters have become heroes, because they shouldnae be held up as role models," said Irvine Welsh. "They should be the reverse. . . . The way people respond to these things tells you about the kind of society we live in now. Ewan McGregor's Renton, to my mind, stands right up there with Robert De Niro's Travis Bickle in *Taxi Driver.*"

Despite all the controversy, *Trainspotting* was an extraordinary success. Even in America, much to the annoyance of the newspaper columnist now known as Martin Scorsese to his pals, it gained a cult following—even if it was appearing in a slightly bastardised form. McGregor and Macdonald's love scene was cut by a few seconds, but, more importantly, the dialogue was changed. Much of the dialogue was based on the dialect used by Welsh in the book—dialogue that most people outside Edinburgh, never mind in America, would have had difficulty understanding. Miramax, the film's US distributor, were deeply concerned when confronted with impenetrable accents uttering phrases like: "ya radge bastard"; "ootae ma visage"; "Oan the other han"; and "haud oot oan us". Macdonald and Miramax quickly agreed dubbed

American voices or English subtitles were not an option. Instead, they used Scottish actors' voices slowed down to an understandable pace.

"We concentrated on the first 20 minutes to give people a chance of getting into it," said Macdonald. "We didn't want them to reject it from the beginning. After that, they either get it or they don't."

In Europe, however, the translations were not always true to the original meaning. In France, for example, to storm off in a "cream puff", slang for huff, became "en piétinant dans les choux de la crème" ("To go away stamping on the cream cakes"), while a "carry oot" (booze from a licensed store) was translated as "sandwiches".

Despite all this, audiences weren't put off. *Trainspotting* made more than $70 million worldwide, and the trade magazine *Variety* called it the most profitable film in the world in 1996.

It became the most successful British film of the year, second only to *Four Weddings and a Funeral* in the all-time list. *Trainspotting* also picked up a number of prestigious awards, and Hodge's screenplay was later nominated for an Oscar. Although considered too controversial to compete officially at Cannes, it was still the most talked-about movie at the film festival.

Accepting an award at a film festival in Scotland, Ewan McGregor joked with the audience when swear words were bleeped out during a clip from the movie. "For those of you who missed it," he said, "the words were fuck, fuck, fucking, fuck and fuck." Afterwards he was approached by an annoyed man in a suit. "This supercilious guy comes up to me and says: 'You've moved away from Scotland so don't come up here and insult us with your foul language.' I told him to fuck off."

The former addicts at Calton Athletic gave the film their blessing and received £25,000 profits from the Scottish premieres. Later, they were given a small percentage of the film's profits. In Scotland, McGregor provided the voice-over for a hard-hitting anti-drugs TV advert.

Trainspotting also made a star of Robert Carlyle, justifiably so, after his unforgettable performance as Begbie. Carlyle's background had helped him understand the character he played so convincingly: "I've met loads of Begbies in my time," he said. "Wander round Glasgow on a Saturday night and you've a good chance of running into Begbie. It was very easy for me to relate to the world of the film. The estate I was brought up on in Glasgow was the Glaswegian equivalent of Leith. A lot of guys from my generation—some of my friends—got involved in the drug scene."

While Boyle, Macdonald and Hodge were hailed as the latest saviours of the British film industry—able to pick and choose the jobs they wanted—Ewan McGregor was beginning to find his star status something of a burden, particularly in view of the media circus surrounding the film's release in the States in July. Hundreds of journalists all wanted to know his views on drugs, and he was sick of it. He may have started out airing those views to just about anyone, but now he had

had enough. The film said more about drugs than he ever could. Full stop. "How about we don't talk about *Trainspotting* at all. So no questions whatsoever. Like, none. OK?"

By the time he appeared on BBC TV's *Parkinson* two years later, the controversy had long since died down, and he clearly felt more relaxed talking about the film. "It's a nightmare of a drug and it's a living hell that these people live," he told Michael Parkinson. "I'm so proud of the film because I think we told the truth, I think we showed the way it is. And of course to begin with, there has got to be some upside to it, otherwise why are people doing it? And I think we were quite brave with that, we showed that. But then of course there is a very quick downward spiral."

It was also the most exhilarating movie he had made to date. "I will never forget making it," he said. "It was film-making in excellence, it really was. That's why it was such a good movie, because of how it was filmed and how it was done. I have never been on a set where it felt like that before. There was a great atmosphere. I was absolutely at ease. There were no egos and that's quite unusual with a bunch of actors."

XIII

How Greenaway Was My Valley

That Hollywood wanted the Trainspotters of Scotland came as no surprise. In the glorious aftermath of *Trainspotting*, Boyle and Macdonald were again being lured by offers from LA, only this time they were major offers. After meeting Sigourney Weaver, Boyle was asked by 20th Century Fox to direct *Alien Resurrection*, the fourth film in the *Alien* saga. He would be paid more than £500,000—an enormous amount for a first-time Hollywood director.

Robert Carlyle was also attracting a massive amount of attention. His compelling performance in *Trainspotting* had received rave reviews. Until then, most people had known him only as the laid-back, dope-smoking rural policeman in the BBC series *Hamish McBeth*.

But it was McGregor who made the greatest impact. Despite the obvious pitfalls of presenting such difficult and often shocking subject matter, he succeeded in portraying Renton as a character with whom the audience could sympathise, even though few were able to identify with his lifestyle. Renton could have been a caricature; McGregor's achievement was to make him human.

Like Gary Oldman and Tim Roth a few years before them, McGregor and Carlyle were being hailed as the latest Brits with the ability to make it big in Hollywood. However, there was one significant difference—the two young Scots had come to prominence primarily because of a renaissance in the British film industry, and the climate in which they flourished was far healthier than that of their predecessors. Oldman and Roth had gone to America because they had no alternative, but for McGregor and Carlyle there seemed to be a choice.

"McGregor and Carlyle inhabit a much more successful industry," said *The Guardian's* film critic Derek Malcolm. "McGregor is undoubtedly a real talent. He was good in *Shallow Grave* but in *Trainspotting* he showed he had matured as an actor."

Trainspotting marked a milestone in British film-making. If *Shallow Grave* had received enthusiastic applause, *Trainspotting* got a standing ovation. In the same way Tarantino went from *Reservoir Dogs* to *Pulp Fiction*, the *Shallow Grave* team progressed with a better, more mature, second film.

Trying to take in the momentous events of the previous year, Andrew Macdonald reflected at the end of 1996: "It has been a pretty amazing year for us. In many ways it couldn't have gone better." McGregor's rise had mirrored theirs—for him it had been a "fucking brilliant year, thank you."

In between *Shallow Grave* and *Trainspotting*, McGregor had worked with Peter Greenaway on *The Pillow Book*, a bizarre erotic fantasy from the controversial director of the extraordinary and beautifully filmed *The Cook, The Thief, His Wife and Her Lover*. *The Pillow Book* was based on a 10th-century text, and featured McGregor as a bisexual translator who accidentally commits suicide, is buried, exhumed, skinned and turned into a book. As far removed from *Trainspotting* as Crieff is from Los Angeles, this film was proof that McGregor would embrace any role if he believed in its quality. While it would be impossible to imagine Tom Cruise in such a part, it merely served to strengthen McGregor's reputation as an actor who could adapt successfully to even the most challenging of roles.

With a budget of only £2 million, *The Pillow Book* was shot on location in Luxembourg, Hong Kong and Japan, at the end of 1994 and beginning of 1995. It was McGregor's first experience of working with Greenaway, a perfectionist whose objectives often seemed wholly different from those of his peers. His films, almost always a visual treat, are not intended for the average multiplex movie fan, being aimed instead at the more cerebral art-house circuit.

The Pillow Book, with its bizarre plot, seemed likely to follow Greenaway's usual pattern. It is a story of sexual power, focusing on the experiences of a Japanese woman, Nagiko (Vivian Wu). One of her earliest memories is of having a traditional birthday greeting painted on her face by her father. But her life has been blighted by her father's relationship with his boss, a homosexual publisher—a relationship to which her father submits in order to obtain money to support his poverty-stricken family. The publisher subsequently forces Nagiko into a loveless marriage with his nephew but, still obsessed by the face-painting ritual, she escapes to Hong Kong, where she seduces a series of calligraphers who paint her body in exchange for sex. She falls in love with Jerome (McGregor), who is keen to learn calligraphy to please her. Nagiko eventually discovers, to her horror, that Jerome is also the lover of the publisher with whom her father was involved.

Jerome then decides to fake suicide in a bid to win Nagiko back, but his plan goes disastrously wrong and he dies. Grief-stricken, Nagiko paints a magnificent love poem on Jerome's body before burying him. The publisher, however, has other ideas—he exhumes the body, cures the skin and produces a book, *The Pillow Book of Jerome*. Nagiko then sends a text, *Book of the Dead*, written on the body of a sumo wrestler, to the publisher, cataloguing his misdeeds. He is forced to give up the *Book of Jerome* before the sumo wrestler slits his throat. Nagiko ritually buries the *Book of Jerome* under a bonsai tree, before continuing the birthday face-painting tradition—this time on her own baby, Jerome's daughter.

"It was unlike anything I've done before," McGregor said afterwards.

The plot may be outlandish, but the performances of McGregor and Wu are compelling. In a film with virtually no dialogue—or costumes—McGregor felt very much an insignificant part of the sweeping vision of a director noted more for the rich visual impact of his films than the details of plot or character. He remembered how Greenaway would set up scenes as though preparing to sit down and paint them on canvas. Such impressionistic direction can leave actors feeling artistically, as well as physically, naked, and it requires true versatility to be able to work successfully within such a framework.

"Greenaway really is an artist," McGregor said, "he paints with the camera. You're as important as the leaves on the tree in the background. A lot of it was hand-held, which surprised me. He'd tell me, 'you come in here and you end up here, and the rest of it is just up to you.' I love that because you really do get a sense of acting, playing around while doing nude scenes, but I'm terrified to see it because I might be really bad. It might be crap. You don't know where to pitch it, how far to push it."

McGregor described the script as one of the most "beautiful" he had seen, full of pages of description. The dialogue was sparse, and the actor even wondered if Greenaway had forgotten to include some. He added: "Then you find out he really didn't bother to write any, but you're doing the scenes so you have to find the dialogue yourself."

If the dialogue was sparse, so were the costumes—Ewan spent most of his time nude in front of the cameras. He would get up at about four every morning to go to a cold studio, and, with only a small heater for warmth, would sleep for two hours as calligraphy was applied to his back. Then he would stand for another two hours while the rest of his body was painted. Often overcome with boredom, he hated the freezing cold of a Luxembourg winter.

On screen, it seemed the cold had no adverse effect on his private parts. Cinema audiences gasped when he revealed all, journalists nervously asked questions about them, and magazines commented on them. *The Face* pronounced McGregor's penis "handsome", while in another interview the actor reasserted his relaxed attitude to displaying his all: "I'm naked a lot of the time, and they don't try to frame potted plants in front of my dick like they do in most other films. It's all part of the story. I've been naked in almost everything I've been in, really. I have it written into my contract."

Chris Heath, writing in the movie magazine *Neon*, asked McGregor: "Do you honestly think you'd do those nude scenes if you had a tiny dick?"

"Don't know," he replied. "I've never had a hang-up about it, and whether that's because I'm pleased with my penis size or not I don't know. I would like to say that of course I would still do it, because it's not a scene about how big or small my dick is, it's a scene about people being naked in a certain situation."

McGregor was also honest enough to admit that rolling about naked with an actress—like Alice Krige in *Scarlet and Black*, or Vivian Wu in *The Pillow Book*—was far from the unpleasant experience claimed by most other performers. He disagreed with the view that actors feel nothing because it is all technical.

"It [is] slightly embarrassing for the first second," he said. "It's more embarrassing for [the crew] who are desperately trying to look like they're not looking at you."

"I actually enjoyed it. Usually you'd get arrested for that sort of thing, but I got paid."

Even so, he is aware of the effect such scenes could have on his relationship with his wife. "It's not easy for her to see things like that," he admitted. "I know I wouldn't like watching her boff someone else on screen. You have to be very careful with each other about that kind of thing, because it hurts. Keep it professional, or keep it in your pants—if you've got any on."

McGregor was also concerned how his parents would feel when they saw their son in such an explicit production. But he needn't have worried—Carol and Jim sent a fax saying how much they enjoyed the film. They thought it was "beautiful". Jim even joked that he now realised why his son was so successful. "I'm glad to see you've inherited one of my major assets," he quipped.

Discussing *The Pillow Book* in *Neon* magazine, McGregor

said: "There's two schools on this one. There's the school that discusses the film's artistic content at great length. And there's the other people that come up and just, straight out, say: 'I saw your cock on screen. I saw your penis four-feet long on a big piece of canvas.'"

The film was released in Britain in the wake of *Trainspotting* towards the end of 1996. It proved a critical success, ultimately showed a modest profit worldwide, and added further to McGregor's ever-increasing army of fans. "McGregor shows that he is one of the cinema's boldest, most charming young actors," concluded *Time* magazine. "It is lovely that, in an age when popular culture dances with the dunces, someone has the urge to parade his intellect, arouse and test his viewers."

Before *Trainspotting*, the creative trio of Boyle, Macdonald and Hodge had grabbed most of the headlines. Now it was McGregor's turn, and *Trainspotting's* publicists cashed in on his popularity by promoting the film largely around his image. His face adorned the covers of numerous youth culture magazines, and his opinions were laid out in detail inside.

Beyond this, the release of two more of his films in the wake of *Trainspotting*—*Emma* and *Brassed Off*—was eagerly awaited. Both had been filmed a year earlier—in the latter half of 1995. McGregor walked from the set of *The Pillow Book* in Luxembourg straight into the media whirlwind that had followed the release of *Shallow Grave*. As an excited public suddenly became aware of his existence, he went north again to join the cast of *Trainspotting*. Then it was off to France to get married, and, after fitting sessions for period costumes, he was back in England on the set of Douglas McGrath's film of the Jane Austen novel, *Emma*.

McGregor was breathless, if not quite speechless. "One minute I was lying on the floor with a syringe in my arm, then I got married, then I was standing in this trailer—I'd never had a big trailer before, it was quite nice—with a wig, and top hat and tails, and leather gloves on, and for a moment I thought: 'I can't go from skinhead drug addict to ha-ha-ha curly wig acting.' "

Perhaps the hectic workload was proving too much, as McGregor proceeded to turn in what some regarded as his worst performance to date.

It may not have been his finest hour, but *Emma* was an overwhelming success when it opened in America. Even President Clinton requested a private screening, at which he sat next to the lead actress Gwyneth Paltrow. Later, he confessed to McGrath he was a Jane Austen fan. When studying at Oxford, he told McGrath, he would "go to tea parties just to listen to the musical way the women spoke, and the film brought that back".

Paltrow may have sat next to the President, but before *Emma* she was better known in Britain as the girlfriend of Brad Pitt than for her acting ability. The decision of the American producers, Miramax, to cast such an apparent lightweight in the role of Austen's matchmaker Emma Woodhouse raised eyebrows, particularly as she had no experience of classical roles.

In Britain, the mood of the critics was sceptical. They were unimpressed by the film, protesting it veered too far away from the original work.

But, against all the odds, Paltrow's finely-balanced performance confounded the sceptics, and she was described by *Time* magazine as "the most elegant actress of her generation". William Russell, in the Glasgow-based *Herald*, referred to a star being born in a film that was badly directed and had a rotten script.

The supporting cast was strong. Toni Collette of *Muriel's Wedding* fame, Greta Scacchi, Juliet Stevenson (*Truly Madly Deeply*), Alan Cumming and Ewan McGregor.

McGregor played Emma's suave suitor Frank Churchill, but he was uncomfortable as the likeable cad. It was a poor performance, and he knew it.

"McGregor looks more like the man with no neck than a sex symbol cad," summed up *The Herald's* William Russell. Those who had worked with him before were in agreement—Chris Kelly, producer on *Kavanagh QC*, who believes McGregor is one of the finest actors of his generation, said: "*Emma* is an example of why I think he has to be a bit more careful. No-one can play everything. In *Emma* he wasn't perhaps cast as accurately as he might have been. I'm sure that's something he would agree with himself."

"My only reservation is that he can't play period," added Otto Plaschkes, his producer on the Screen One comedy *Doggin' Around*. "He's not very good at it. It's something to do with the space, something to do with how you carry yourself. Ewan is relaxed in modern parts, in the Gap look of jeans and T-shirts, but not in tight-fitting breeches."

Although McGregor may disagree with those who claim he is unsuited to period parts in general, while making *Emma* he was fully aware of the awkwardness of his performance. He later admitted that, so soon after the rigours of *Trainspotting* and getting married, he had not been fully committed to the project: "I never read the novel," he said. "I think the film's all right but I was so crap, I was terrible in it. I didn't believe a word I said. I just thought: 'Shut the fuck up, Frank.' It was the first time for me. I was really embarrassed about it, and I'm not paranoid about that usually. But this time I didn't know what I was doing. . . . I was under the fucking sofa when I was watching *Emma*." He said he concentrated so hard on mastering a "clipped" English accent that he forgot about everything else.

"It's all right to do a bad one," he reassured himself. "We'll move on."

McGregor did exactly that, immediately. He rushed straight from the set of *Emma* to the former mining village of Grimethorpe in Yorkshire to film a small but ambitious British production, *Brassed Off*. The rest of the cast had already been on set for a week—including Pete Postlethwaite (*In the Name of the Father, The Usual Suspects*), Stephen Tompkinson (*Ballykissangel, Drop the Dead Donkey*) and Tara Fitzgerald (*Sirens, The Camomile Lawn*), as well as members of the Grimethorpe Colliery Band.

Writer and director Mark Herman had taken a gamble by

agreeing that McGregor could have such a short change-over, as any hold-up on *Emma* would have played havoc with his limited budget. Fortunately, McGregor's timing was impeccable. In his trailer on the set of *Emma* he had learned the script for his next film, and listened intently to tapes of Yorkshire accents in order to develop his own for his part as the young miner Andy.

"Coming straight off the set of *Emma* to *Brassed Off* was quite remarkable," said one movie insider. "Everyone had been quite nervous about the arrangement but he came and he walked right into a chip shop scene which he handled superbly. There was no chance of breaking in gently, he was straight in at the deep end. His accent even sounded natural. It takes a special kind of quality to pull it off the way he did."

If *Emma* was McGregor's worst moment, the critically acclaimed black comedy *Brassed Off* was undoubtedly one of his finest. It is a charming film based on the trials and tribulations of a Yorkshire mining community and the local colliery's brass band. (McGregor used his French horn experience at Morrison's Academy to "tootle along" during the brass band scenes.) As the mine faces closure, the band is on the way to the final of a national competition. Postlethwaite is outstanding as the terminally-ill conductor Danny who persuades and cajoles his musicians into keeping going as their lives begin to fall apart. His son Phil (Tompkinson) tries to fight off loan sharks by moonlighting disastrously as a clown—Mr Chuckles—at children's Christmas parties. Later, in the depths of despair, he votes for redundancy and tries to kill himself.

McGregor's character, Andy, becomes involved romantically with the new female member of the band, and former school girlfriend, played by Fitzgerald. However, unknown to Andy and the rest of the band, she is working for the management—who are intent on closing the pit. In real life McGregor and Fitzgerald were friends, and the film's romantic scenes, she later confided, were "more mates than passion."

McGregor had been attracted to Herman's script because he sympathised with the portrayal of a community, and a country in general, reeling from the effects of almost two decades of Conservative rule. "People got fed up with that bunch," he said shortly after the Labour Party's general election victory in May 1997. "All I know is it can't be any worse than it was. I've got a feeling Labour cares, and I know for a fact the Tory party just couldn't give a shit."

But the shoot itself turned out to be a bleak experience, bringing McGregor face-to-face with the grim legacy of Thatcherism. "I saw three-bedroomed houses for sale for £5,000, people desperately trying to get out of there. And you can't do that. If you're going to take away people's livelihoods, you have to replace it with something. I was there for seven weeks and at the end I was just so saddened by it all that I was dying to get away."

XIV

FAMILY TIES

In 1996, Ewan McGregor's fans were spoilt for choice, as he starred in four acclaimed movies—*Trainspotting*, *Emma*, *The Pillow Book* and *Brassed Off*. He was approaching the top of the acting tree, and was rapidly becoming master of his own destiny. But that year his spectacular career take-off was eclipsed by the most important event in his life to date—the birth of his daughter, Clara.

Eve became pregnant in the summer of 1995. Her sister Marianne has described her as an outgoing woman who was determined to succeed in her career, but who wanted, more than anything else, to be a mother.

In February 1996, a beautiful baby girl was born in a

London hospital, and the proud parents named their new daughter Clara Mathilde McGregor. Her dad, who was just 24, remembered the day as the most frightening of his life. When Eve's contractions suddenly started in the middle of the night, the young couple rushed from their flat on the edge of Regent's Park. Shortly beforehand, in an interview with *Premiere* magazine to promote the forthcoming *Trainspotting*, the stress was clearly taking its toll on the actor. He was described as looking terrible: "pale, slightly puffy face, pinkish eyes, blemishes". "I'm falling to bits," he admitted. "The anticipation is killing me."

On arrival at the hospital, he was suddenly gripped by feelings of terror. "I wasn't prepared to be frightened," he said. "I imagined you had to be this rock for your wife, and I just got more and more frightened the longer it went on, that something was going to go wrong. In the end she had a Caesarean section, and I had to go in there and all I was thinking was: 'Oh no, I'm not big enough for this, not quite sure if I can handle this one.'"

Following the traumatic birth, McGregor returned home alone to the flat they had left two days before—and began to contemplate life as a father. It was the middle of the night, but he began phoning relatives to tell them the news. "I phoned a lot of people, crying down the phone to my parents (screeching and wailing)," he recalled. "And they were like . . . (screeching and wailing). Lots of crying people. Lots of people asleep as well. (Bleary voice:) 'Oh that's good, that's good.' (Shouting:) 'No, but I just went through this thing.' (Bleary voice:) 'Aye, anyway, I'll speak to you later, it's five in the morning.' "

McGregor was unsure how he would take to the addition of another human being in his extraordinarily busy life, especially one who would naturally become the centre of his priorities.

The responsibility and commitment required now were in complete contrast to the lifestyle he had led when he arrived in London almost seven years earlier. It may have taken a while for him to get used to the hustle and bustle of one of the world's biggest cities, but he soon came to regard it as home. To begin with he had lived the life of a student—in the YMCA, then the flats in Hackney and Leytonstone. As he matured, so did his tastes. Immersing himself in London's cultural diversity, he fell in love with the enormous variety of theatres, music venues, art galleries, museums and parks at his disposal. London stimulated his imagination in a way that no other city could—satisfying the longing to be different that had existed from such an early age in Crieff.

In 1992, while working on *Lipstick On Your Collar*, McGregor had moved into a rented bachelor pad in Primrose Hill in north London. His flat was on the first floor of a Victorian terrace block in an area well known for its relaxed upmarket atmosphere.

The small curving street on which he lived, Regent's Park Road, was notable for its rows of once-luxurious town-houses painted in a range of pastel colours—yellows, pinks, purples and blues—shadowed by mature trees that lined the wide pavements. There were numerous boutiques, restaurants and cafes, lending the area a distinctly European feel. Only five minutes' walk away was the Bohemia of Camden's markets, restaurants and bars, and just around the corner was the flat of one of his best actor friends, Jude Law.

The high rent may have stretched the young actor's limited finances, but the laid-back atmosphere and convenience of the area more than compensated for this. Directly opposite was a delicatessen, a hairdresser, and a fish and chip shop. More important, perhaps, were the two off-licences and a pub. One of his locals, The Engineer, just a few minutes' walk away, was well-known as a haven for actors. At night, he loved to venture into Soho, a once-seedy area associated with prostitutes and peep-shows that had cleaned up its image in the early 1990s with an influx of new bars, restaurants and clubs.

Ewan McGregor had enjoyed being young and single for most of the time he lived in the flat, but after meeting Eve in 1994 he was ready to settle down. In due course, the shopkeepers who had often seen McGregor on his own nursing a hangover were now getting used to the sight of him pushing his daughter in her pram.

Though neither London's richest nor trendiest area, it was one the couple were sad to leave. But a bachelor flat was too small for a family of three, and they wanted a larger home with a garden so Clara would have room to play. They finally paid a reported £1.25 million for a town-house on the edge of nearby St John's Wood and Belsize Park.

Friends said McGregor brought in a firm of architects to help redesign and convert some of the rooms—Eve's aptitude as a designer and Ewan's enthusiasm helped the professionals transform the property, creating the feel the couple desired.

While on screen McGregor explored the more extreme sides of life in films like *Trainspotting* and *The Pillow Book*, his real-life existence was mundane by comparison, most of his spare time being devoted to his new family, and the occasional round of golf.

But although the responsibilities of marriage, fatherhood and celebrity curtailed his night-time visits to Soho, he still loved going out. Like most men of his age, he got drunk with his mates, staggered home, and woke up the following morning with a hangover.

"It's pretty common knowledge that I spend half of my free time drinking and the other half dealing with my hangovers," he joked. "It's not a lifestyle I recommend, but it's mine." "I'm drunk so often," he told another interviewer. "They're not big stories any more, it's just a state of being for me. I've yet to be found in a gutter somewhere. I always get away with it somehow."

Eve, on the other hand, preferred the comforts of home. She and Clara were often already in bed when Ewan came in at night, and still asleep when he left early the next morning to go to a film set. "I think differences work out," he said. "Maybe people who are the same shouldn't really live together."

McGregor finally took time out from his gruelling schedule

at the beginning of 1997 for a three-month break with his family. But the holiday quickly turned into one of the worst periods of his life, when Clara was struck down by meningitis.

The youngster battled for weeks against the illness, which affects the brain and is potentially fatal in young children. Her parents could only look on helpless. Fortunately, Clara pulled through and eventually made a complete recovery, but the scare hammered home the fragility of a young child, and put her father's successful existence clearly into perspective.

"The best thing about the year was my baby coming through that," he recalled afterwards. "It's the scariest thing that has ever happened, and the happiest."

Later that year, because of his wife's work commitments, Ewan spent a week on his own with Clara for the first time at his parents' home in Perthshire. He was just grateful she was still around to be there with him, and looked back on the break as one of the happiest periods of his life. A closer bond than ever before was established between father and daughter. "I don't live the rock 'n' roll life," he said. "It's not something I've ever wanted. I'm a married man with a family and I'm completely happy with that. I love Clara to bits."

"People might not like to hear this but Ewan is just a really nice guy who doesn't give a shit about this fame thing," said a friend. "His ambitions are to do the best he can as an actor, not to become a star. He has never been like that and never will be. He has got pals he gets drunk with, he had girl-friends then he got married, and now he has got a baby.

The meningitis thing scared the wits out of him. He would have been totally wrecked had Clara not come through that. Marriage might mean a high level of commitment, but he enjoys the stability that comes with it."

The proud father said the arrival of his daughter was the best thing that ever happened to him. But both parents realised early on that Ewan's career commitments had the potential to put a severe strain on their marriage. "There are a lot of wrecked marriages in this business and we didn't want ours to be one," he said. "So we made a pact to always travel together, which we do."

Eve and Clara went just about everywhere with the actor, even on film sets, where their company was often written into his contracts. Sometimes Eve's mother Annie Joelle joined them too—on a McGregor set, it would often be a real family affair. "Our mum goes to see Ewan, Eve and the baby in the holidays and sometimes she goes to see them on the movie sets," said Marianne. "Ewan is very mature with a sense of responsibility. He's a really good daddy. He's also a really good husband. Eve and Ewan love each other dearly. On one occasion she was working in Kenya on a shoot. He loved her so much he flew out to be with her because he could not bear to spend a weekend away from her.

"She wants to do new things. She's not content with staying at home bringing up babies. The most important thing is that she is with Ewan. He makes sure the family spend as much time together by the fact that they go everywhere together."

If McGregor was only away for a couple of weeks he went alone, but on longer shoots the family always travelled together. "He's totally wrapped up in Eve and Clara," said a friend. "But he believes it's not fair to bring a baby halfway round the world if it's only for a relatively short time."

"I'm lucky my family comes with me wherever I go," said McGregor in 1996. "Travelling takes its toll and we've moved around a lot in the last two years, but I'd go bananas without them."

The idea of one of the world's top twenty-something stars walking around a movie set with his baby daughter on his back may seem strange, but McGregor had long ago rejected the stereotypical lifestyle of many of his peers. According to friends, his wife and child are the focus of his life—his home, and that of his parents, are filled with family pictures, and his relationship with Eve is conducted on equal terms, with both partners shouldering the responsibilities.

"I don't think I have ever seen such a devoted father," said Jim McGregor. "He does everything—even changes the nappies. Success hasn't changed him a bit."

"How did fatherhood change you?" Ewan was once asked.

"In the same way it would change anyone's life when they become a father."

"And how's that?"

"Very little sex."

If McGregor sometimes resented the restrictions imposed on him by his celebrity status, Eve was even less keen to play the role of the celebrity wife. She had her own ambitions within the film industry, and wanted a successful career of her own. Usually she stood back from the public gaze, content to let her husband enjoy the limelight. He happily posed for publicity shots—but never with Eve or Clara, and he seldom released family pictures to the media. The images that appeared in magazines were usually photos taken when the family were out in public. Perhaps his reluctance was fuelled by a women's magazine that referred to his "fashion-accessory wife and child". "That's disgusting actually, isn't it?" he said.

He coped with the intense media interest, but his family were kept off-limits. "I'm private in terms of my family," said McGregor, "and I don't like people sticking their nose into that." Intimate occasions like family birthdays, for example, were celebrated privately. "They don't necessarily have a big party," said Marianne, "but they will buy each other presents that are of great personal significance. One Christmas Ewan bought Eve a piano. She used to play the piano as a child and he realised how much something like that would mean to her. It was such a wonderful gift, the present of her dreams."

"No-one is more thrilled about how well Ewan has done than Ewan himself," said one friend. "But the intrusion and questioning that comes with it does bother him. He does a job like anyone else, albeit more high-profile. Why should he talk about stuff that's got absolutely nothing to do with his acting? It's no-one's business what he does, especially if it has anything to do with Eve or Clara."

Those who crossed the line were met with a frosty response. When Clara had meningitis a journalist from the *News of the World*—Britain's biggest-selling Sunday newspaper—appeared on his doorstep asking about her welfare. McGregor sent him packing in no uncertain terms. On another occasion, an interviewer from *The Times* asked if he had paid £1.25 million for his new house. McGregor replied: "None of your business."

"He doesn't like people peering into his private life and that's natural," said the friend. "Anyone would feel the same way. He especially dislikes people wanting to know how much money he has spent on this, or earned on that. He realises they are going to be interested in his affairs because of what he is, he just doesn't enjoy the intrusion."

Lou Reed, whose haunting "Perfect Day" accompanied McGregor's performance as Renton overdosing in *Trainspotting*, was once asked what he would regard as the lowest depth of misery. "Being interviewed by an English journalist," he replied.

McGregor's opinion of the press was not as extreme, but he understood the sentiment. The actor still had reservations about the number of media interviews he was required to do to promote films, and was particularly wary of the tendency of the tabloid press in Britain to pick up on off-the-cuff remarks, then blow them up out of all proportion.

Following *Trainspotting*, every reporter on the planet seemed to want an insight into McGregor's most intimate thoughts. After speaking to dozens of journalists in one day, he recalled how he was "dribbling" by the final interview.

In general, though, McGregor came across well in interviews. Journalists who met him were always struck by how friendly, funny and charming he was.

"He was superb," said one impressed hack. "To be honest, in a business packed full of ignorant prima donnas and wannabees he was a breath of fresh air. He was such a lovely guy."

McGregor's charm was that of a character who enjoyed his elevated status, did not take himself too seriously, and possessed a self-deprecating sense of humour that often came to the fore in interviews.

Charming though he may have been, he was also excellent at "staying on message". Like most well-trained stars, he chatted amiably, told journalist after journalist virtually the same thing, and rarely gave anything away. "People will do anything, it seems, to be a big movie star. I don't understand what that's about. I want to spend my efforts making my life the way it should be, instead of trying to spend my energy getting my life in the media."

"He has always wanted to be an actor, not a movie star," said another friend. "Being an actor was a very real thing for him. If the truth be told, he would prefer not to be famous."

Acting was his life—but he derived little pleasure from the public baggage that came with it. He hated being described as "hip", an "icon" of his generation or, worse, a hero. "Hero? A symbol of our times perhaps, but not a hero," he reflected.

Most sympathised with McGregor's reaction to the negative aspects of celebrity status. But at a time when TV and film-world celebrities appear to have replaced government and church leaders as the figures people look up to, the media was merely fuelling a voracious public appetite.

"It's like asking, do you think of yourself as a sexy person," said McGregor, commenting on what he thought of being regarded as a sex symbol. "I don't waste my time imagining myself as these things. They are things people can think of you as."

And they do. According to a recent poll in the US magazine *Glamour*, McGregor is the man most American women want to get between the sheets. His "cute looks and sexy Scottish accent" even edged out Johnny Depp and Leonardo DiCaprio. Meanwhile, in Britain, the April 1998 edition of *Company* announced that McGregor's appendage had come out tops in the magazine's "Man Oscars". He won the award for Best Full Frontal for his 38 seconds of complete nudity in *The Pillow Book*, beating off rival contenders Richard Gere and Max Beesley. Deciding that the calligraphy-dominated film must have provided the hottest make-up artist's job in town, *Company* said McGregor won "simply because it's Ewan-Call-Me-Sex-God-McGregor, and the scene is certainly the longest in all senses of the word. Plus, anyone who can make ginger pubic hair look sexy deserves an Oscar."

"The thing that surprises my fans most about me is that I'm an old married man," he said. "People get incredibly rude about it sometimes. They really expect me to be like the character I usually play. I hope those people get a chance to see me in *Brassed Off* because I play closer to the real me than I've done before."

The most important things in McGregor's life are his family, his friends and the movies. His other great love is motorbikes. He owned an old Motoguzzi, and more recently bought a £15,000 Ducati 748. One of his dreams is to own a racing team, and in 1998 he tested a racing bike at Brands Hatch. At some point he hopes to ride alone through Europe and Africa, attracted by the prospect of the anonymity of the road: "Who's going to know who I am?"

But such dreams were becoming increasingly unattainable. After *Trainspotting*, McGregor was deluged with offers to make movies in Hollywood. This, he knew, was a dangerous route to travel—especially for an actor accustomed to choosing parts for their quality, rather than the financial rewards that went with them. Countless British actors before him had been sucked into the American movie machine, only to be spat out again unceremoniously. At the same time, McGregor knew he had to expand his horizons beyond Britain if he was to find new acting challenges.

At home, he had the full support of his wife in choosing his next movie role. They both read the scripts on offer and discussed their merits, although ultimately the final decision would rest with the actor. "He goes for quality scripts," said Eve's sister Marianne. "They will discuss them together but he will always make the final choice."

McGregor finally chose *Nightwatch* as his first Hollywood

venture. It was being made by Dimension Films, a division of Miramax.

He went to America with no desire to live the claustrophobic lifestyle of the Los Angeles film scene, believing it infinitely preferable to arrive just in time to start a picture, and then jump on a plane as soon as it was finished.

"When I met with agents in LA, they would tell me that you had to do two movies for yourself and then two for the business," he said. "And I thought: 'Fuck off, no you don't.' You do every film because you want to do good work. Because you're interested in making good movies and working with good people. To do a crappy event movie for a lot of money, like *Independence Day*, I would never taint my soul with that crap."

It was a principled stand. But only time would tell if it was a realistic position for a young actor on his way to Hollywood.

XV

TINSELTOWN

Shortly after the birth of his daughter, Ewan McGregor entered the lion's den—flying to Los Angeles to make his first feature film in Hollywood.

Trainspotting had yet to be released in the States, but the executives at Miramax were confident its massive success in Britain would ensure a cult following across the Atlantic. They also felt certain McGregor—an unknown in America at that time—would become the focus of that interest.

The new film, *Nightwatch*, a thriller being made by Dimension Films, would feature McGregor alongside well-known stars like Nick Nolte and Patricia Arquette. It was hoped the role would be the perfect follow-up to

Trainspotting, establishing him as a mainstream box-office draw in America.

McGregor's relationship with Miramax was already well established. He had originally been noticed by the company's two top men, Bob and Harvey Weinstein, on the set of *Scarlet and Black* three years earlier, and Miramax had since been involved in a number of his projects, including *Shallow Grave*, *Brassed Off*, *Trainspotting* and *Emma*.

The *Nightwatch* shoot lasted two months. McGregor was cast as Martin Belos, a law student who takes a job as a part-time security guard in a morgue. Around the same time, a serial killer starts terrorising the city. Nick Nolte plays Inspector Cray, the detective hunting the killer. Cray discovers that all the clues lead back to Martin—who becomes the prime suspect.

The film was a $10 million remake of the Danish thriller *Nattevagten*, and the director, Ole Bornedal, also made the original. Arquette plays the part of McGregor's girlfriend, Katherine, but they met only briefly, as they completed their scenes together in the first week. He got on well with Nolte, and overall he enjoyed making the film. But when *Nightwatch* was released in America in April 1998, the critics were scathing. According to G. Allen Johnson of the *San Francisco Examiner*, "Ole Bornedal, in remaking his own European art-house hit, presents us with pretty pictures and one of the most boring lead characters in quite a long time. And considering the lead is played by Ewan McGregor, the hot Scottish import who simply dazzled in *Trainspotting* and *The*

Pillow Book, that's quite an achievement." Another reviewer described the cast's performances as "terrible across the board," adding: "Maybe it's a great film in Denmark, but it's a terrible, terrible movie in America."

McGregor's experience on *Nightwatch* only served to strengthen his suspicion of the world's movie-making capital:

"I don't like the way the business is run," he said. "It's not about anything that I'm involved in really. It's not the actors or the people of LA, they are all very nice people. But the people who run the business there, executives and studios I'm talking about really. There are as many good American independent film-makers as there are anywhere else. But the studio system is so lost, I think, and the films that are being made by them are, on the whole, really dire. I speak to the people there, and they don't get it. They talk about A-lists and B-lists in casting. Who cares? Who's best for the fucking part? Well we don't know, we need an A-list. No, who's best for the fucking part? They don't get it. So I'm certainly not going to make any effort to crack it. I'm quite happy where I am, doing what I'm doing."

McGregor's attitude to Hollywood seems to have been a mixture of idealism and good old-fashioned cynicism. In many ways the major studios represented everything he didn't. For their executives, the most important thing when making a movie was money. The bigger the star, the bigger the takings at the box office. McGregor, on the other hand, always valued the quality of the product above the potential rewards—he went for scripts because his gut instinct told

21ST CENTURY BOY—AT THE PREMIERE OF THE
SPECIAL EDITION OF *STAR WARS*, 20TH MARCH 1997

ON SET WITH ANNA FRIEL IN A SCENE FROM *ROGUE TRADER*

'SHE'S THE BEST'—CAMERON DIAZ AND EWAN IN *A LIFE LESS ORDINARY* (1997)

'WE WENT DOWN LIKE A
BUCKET OF COLD SICK'
EWAN WITH CAMERON DIAZ
AT THE MTV MOVIE AWARDS,
8TH JUNE 1997

ABOVE: WITH EVE AND CLARA, CANNES, MAY 1996
BELOW: AT A CHARITY FOOTBALL MATCH, JUNE 1997

BELOW: PICKING UP AN AWARD AT THE SPFF, FEBRUARY 1997

ABOVE: 'I WANTED TO BE DIFFERENT, LIKE HIM'—EWAN WITH DENIS LAWSON, FEBRUARY 1998
BELOW: EVE, CAROL, EWAN AND JIM AT THE 1997 SCOTTISH BAFTA CEREMONY

'USUALLY YOU'D GET ARRESTED FOR THAT SORT OF THING, BUT I GOT PAID'
THE PILLOW BOOK (1996)

STEPHEN TOMPKINSON AND EWAN MCGREGOR IN *BRASSED OFF* (1996)

THE
RA

ABOVE: EWAN WITH PAUL MYLES (LEFT), DUCATI LAUNCH, BRANDS HATCH, FEBRUARY 1998
BELOW: MY NAME IS MICHAEL CAINE—EWAN AND FANS, GLASGOW, FEBRUARY 1998

him to, and was happiest working with people he knew and trusted.

Following the success of *Trainspotting*, executives from Hollywood approached McGregor en masse, hoping to entice him into starring in their next project. Yet before *Nightwatch* he had refused all of them, because the scripts were not up to the standard he sought. He maintained he would do a film anywhere, including Hollywood, if the script was good enough—but as far as he was concerned, Hollywood rarely offered the quality he was used to in Britain.

After *Trainspotting*, Ewan McGregor and Robert Carlyle were widely regarded as the most promising British actors since Gary Oldman and Tim Roth rose to prominence in the late eighties. But if Channel 4 had not triggered a resurgence in the British film industry by deciding to back low-budget films, McGregor would probably have failed to get his big break in the first place. Films like *Shallow Grave* and *Trainspotting* would never have been made. As it was, however, Ewan was at the centre of a revolution—he was the hottest British actor in a vibrant industry that was making an unprecedented 120 films a year. And as a result he had the pick of all the best scripts.

Hardly surprising, then, that McGregor was a staunch supporter of the British film industry: "We have got really good writers here, incredible facilities, the best technicians in the world and we make really good movies. The quality of our work is far superior."

"Channel 4 saved the British film industry," said *The*

Guardian's film critic Derek Malcolm. "It all means actors have a much better chance of being noticed in America and in Europe. A few years ago Gary Oldman and Tim Roth went to America because they were getting nowhere in England, despite doing very good work. That was the only alternative they had. Ewan McGregor and Bobby Carlyle are the Tim Roths and Gary Oldmans of their day. They inhabit a much more successful industry. I don't mean the films are better but there are more of them. They get better publicity and they are more widely shown in the States in particular. There's a good chance, therefore, of them becoming taste of the year. That is exactly what happened to Ewan McGregor after *Trainspotting*. The key is that Britain can now make films about its own culture and they will be a success in America."

Malcolm, however, was less enthusiastic about McGregor's desire to take on Hollywood on his own terms. "He's got to decide whether he wants to be in big popular films where he will use about 50 per cent of his ability or smaller more intelligent films out of which he will get a good deal more than that. He may wish to try to do both but that's very difficult. It never works that way. Actors think they can do it, but in reality very few people can do what Anthony Hopkins did. He was able to charge very little money to do a British film, but a lot of money for a Hollywood film. Generally actors get sucked into the system and they have to decide whether they want to be a star actor or an actor star."

Oldman's experience of Hollywood seemed to be the most relevant comparison with McGregor's predicament. Oldman had left Britain in the early nineties with hopes of cracking the American market, while at the same time maintaining his artistic integrity. His performances there initially won widespread praise, but roles in action movies like *Air Force One* and *The Fifth Element* left him disillusioned with Hollywood. He returned to Britain in 1997 to make his directorial debut, the critically-acclaimed low-budget British film *Nil By Mouth*. "I said in effect, Fuck America," he commented later. "I got into a bit of a rut with typecasting. I started not to take myself, or my career, very seriously."

So far, McGregor had avoided such problems. Rather, he was being hailed as Britain's most versatile actor since Daniel Day Lewis. Then again, Oldman had been described in similar terms when he set out for America. "Ewan is an actor whose potential has yet to be fulfilled," said Malcolm, "roughly in the way Gary Oldman's potential was yet to be fulfilled before he went to America. Now, of course it has been fulfilled in the wrong way. He has just become a parody of himself in America, he knows it and that's why he's making films now.

"It would be absolutely accurate to say that Ewan is in a position rather like Gary Oldman. Ewan might find that he will be sucked into being a star rather than an actor. That happened to Oldman. He says he is bored with acting now. What he actually means is he is bored with acting in shitty parts. Gary came back to London to make *Nil By Mouth* and that was his crowning achievement, really, after years in Hollywood. It was remarkable."

McGregor, however, seemed intent on avoiding LA—

unless he could work there on his own terms. Perhaps he was remembering the words of Dennis Potter, who told him that all the shit eventually floats to the top in Tinseltown. Or maybe it was symptomatic of an individual who naturally rebelled against authority. He had walked away from the school that would not allow him to study his favourite subjects, he still felt passionately about being rejected from RADA because of his age, and, just as he had wanted to be different as a young boy in Crieff, he had no desire now to travel the accepted route to movie stardom.

"I've always thought you could have it both ways," he said, adding that he would shoot himself in the head before getting involved with a big budget movie like *Independence Day*.

Before starting to shoot *Nightwatch*, he told one interviewer how he believed talent had played no part in his being offered the role. They wanted him in the film "So they can put on their poster, 'Ewan McGregor from *Shallow Grave*'," he said. "You do wonder, how much of it is about me. And I know I should grow up about it, really. But I've done so many meetings over there where they've said, 'Of course, we want a big American name for this part.' Well I've got a big Scottish name. Fuckin' use mine," he said, only half joking.

Few Brits before him had mastered the Hollywood way of doing business. Hugh Grant was the most notable recent casualty. He went to Hollywood after the astonishing success of *Four Weddings and a Funeral* but fell out of favour almost immediately—although he did achieve a certain notoriety as a result of his performance with Divine Brown on Sunset

Boulevard. Only Anthony Hopkins and Sean Connery could claim to have made it into the major league—the latter had just landed a pay cheque of $12.5 million for his role alongside Nicholas Cage in the action movie *The Rock*. Now McGregor was being touted as the heir apparent to Connery's crown. As one American producer told *The Sunday Times*: "He's totally hot. He really has a shot and he's young."

"It's all there for him, if he wants it," said *Brassed Off* director Mark Herman. "[But] I hope he stays [in the UK]. He seems to think the work is over here, which is good to see. It's about time somebody stayed."

By the end of the *Nightwatch* shoot McGregor's opinion of Hollywood remained unaltered. In LA, he concluded, there were movies, and absolutely nothing else. "I don't know what I'd do if I wasn't working in LA," he told one interviewer. "I think I'd probably go out of my brain. If you stayed there you would just dry up."

"One thing is certain, I'll never live in LA, if I can get away with it, and I can."

As if to emphasise his unwillingness to accept the Hollywood route to stardom, McGregor returned home to begin work on three projects totally removed from the excesses of Tinseltown: a pan-European funded movie, a short made by one of his friends, and a film made in America by a British team. One could almost see him sticking two fingers up at the Hollywood establishment.

His first stop was the village of Sixmilebridge in County Clare, Ireland, for a two-month shoot on the $13 million period drama, *The Serpent's Kiss*. The cast was impressive, including Pete Postlethwaite, Greta Scacchi and Richard E. Grant. The director Philippe Rousselot had won an Oscar for his cinematography on *A River Runs Through It*, and producer Robert Jones was a veteran of *The Usual Suspects*. Funding for the movie came primarily from the UK, France and Germany.

McGregor had agreed to take the lead role after reading Tim Rose Price's screenplay nine months earlier. The film is set in Gloucestershire in 1699, and McGregor plays a Dutch landscape gardener, Meneer Chrome, who is employed by pompous landowner Thomas Smithers (Postlethwaite) to create a garden in celebration of the beauty of his bored wife Juliana, played by Scacchi. As the project takes on outlandish proportions, she falls for Chrome. He in turn falls for her daughter, and Juliana's distant cousin Fitzmaurice arrives on the scene to cause no end of trouble. Eventually, Chrome is blackmailed by the jealous cousin and a tale of sexual intrigue and deceit unfolds.

The film took over the small Irish village for three months in the summer of 1996, and cast members were often to be found in Paddy Casey's, the local pub, still dressed in costume. During the day Ewan filmed mainly at the beautiful 17th-century stately home, Mount Eivers House, while at night he often sat outside his hotel with his wife and daughter, enjoying the peace and tranquillity and the company of his family. "It was a very relaxed shoot, but hard work at the same time," said producer Robert Jones. "That is the way I like it. Everyone in the village got into the spirit of the thing. We made a lot of friends and one publican very rich."

Jones said McGregor could easily have walked away from the project, as he had plenty of offers to shoot other more lucrative films at the same time. "We got such a good cast on the quality of the script," he said. "Ewan stayed loyal in the face of bigger offers. He committed a good six to eight months before the film was shot. In that time there were a lot of people after him for other things. He stayed very true to it." McGregor was enthusiastic about the script. "I'm passionate about it," he said. "It's one of the best I've read in a long time and it's beautifully written."

During filming co-star Richard E. Grant commented on the huge interest surrounding McGregor: "[He is] astonishingly grounded. Considering the career tornado around him, it's amazing his head doesn't turn 360 degrees."

Robert Jones thought McGregor was incredibly focused and hard-working. "The first time I saw him in *Lipstick On Your Collar* he immediately just stood out as being someone who had a presence. I think there are similarities between him and a young Albert Finney. He's a bit of a rogue, he's very likeable and cheeky. But he has a real believability. It helps if you are an actor and you are instantly likeable. Even if he plays characters that aren't 100 per cent sympathetic, there is just a quality that allows him to get away with it because you kind of forgive them. The eyes are important, the smile too. He's very personable, and he is a very genuine bloke in real life. I do think that comes across."

"I think he gives a very good performance [in *The Serpent's Kiss*]," added Jones, rejecting the theory that McGregor wasn't cut out for period roles. "We didn't want the film to be mannered in the way a lot of period films are. That's another reason Ewan is interesting in the part, because there is a modern quality about him."

In September 1996, Ewan McGregor returned to London to record a voice-over for Virgin Atlantic, before going to Eastbourne in southern England to begin his next project. He had agreed to a five-night shoot for a short film, *Swimming With The Fishes*, a tale of sexual intrigue set in a fish and chip shop, directed by his friend Justin Chadwick.

By this time he was arguably Britain's biggest young star, but still found time to help out friends like Chadwick. They had worked together previously in 1993 on another short film, *Family Style*. Written by 18-year-old Matthew Cooper, *Family Style* was an eleven-minute black and white film for Channel 4 that was part of the Lloyd's Bank Young Writers' Challenge. In the film, McGregor plays a Yorkshire teenager coming to terms with a bereavement. At that time the actor had still been struggling to establish himself, and the difficult period that followed *Lipstick On Your Collar* was fresh in his mind. Now, in September 1996, he was back helping Chadwick once more, describing his involvement as a "weird loyalty thing".

After finishing *Swimming With The Fishes*, McGregor was hoping for a well-earned break with his wife and daughter before heading off to America for his next project.

But the makers of *Nightwatch* upset those plans. They needed him back in LA for reshooting. The two days he had set aside for a holiday were the only time he could do it.

"Fucking bastards," he told interviewer Sylvia Paterson. "Why didn't they fucking notice this three months ago? And they do it very cleverly, try and make it seem advantageous to you, which of course is fucking rubbish, and all that flattery doesn't mean a fucking thing to me. Och, (deep sigh) I understand, though—it happens."

The problems with *Nightwatch* would soon be forgotten, however, as McGregor was about to team up with the creators of *Shallow Grave* and *Trainspotting* for their third project together. Once again, the Trainspotters were going to spring a surprise—their new project was a romantic comedy. And although it was a British film, they were going to make it in America.

XVI

A LIFE LESS USUAL

Somewhere between the peaks of *Shallow Grave* and *Trainspotting*, John Hodge sat down to write another script. Provisionally entitled *A Life Less Usual*, it was essentially a road movie set in France and Scotland. Eighteen rewrites later it had become *A Life Less Ordinary*, and was now set in Utah, in the heart of the American Bible Belt. The plot itself was deeply unconventional, focusing on the character of Robert, a young Scots drifter working in America as a cleaner. Outraged at being sacked and replaced by a robot, Robert kidnaps his boss's spoiled daughter, and then robs a bank.

Meanwhile, Danny Boyle and Andrew Macdonald had been fielding the many lucrative offers that came in the wake of *Trainspotting's* success. One of these looked particularly promising—*Alien Resurrection*, the fourth movie in the *Alien* series, which 20th Century Fox wanted them to make. They liked the script and Boyle was even offered £500,000 to direct it. He looked set to become a major Hollywood player, and the British movie industry mourned the imminent loss of one of the architects of its latest revolution.

But Macdonald and Boyle, renowned for their unpredictability in the past, had another surprise up their sleeve. They passed on the $70 million blockbuster, and went instead to Utah to shoot their third Hodge screenplay. Defying the conventions of big studio movie-making, they opted for the total control that came with their lower budget alternative. "After a few meetings, Danny and I realised *Alien 4* wasn't the kind of film we wanted to do," said Macdonald.

Once that decision had been made, they started the search for the $12 million they needed to make *A Life Less Ordinary*. Macdonald approached Channel 4 first, primarily out of appreciation for the support they had shown in the past. He knew Channel 4 would be unable to finance the project on their own, but he wanted them involved anyway. In return, Channel 4 provided Macdonald with enough cash to go to America to seek out major backers. Ironically, he found that the same executives who had offered him *Alien Resurrection* were willing to fund his movie. Even more remarkably, 20th Century Fox agreed not to interfere with the making of the film until the final cut arrived on their desks. Boyle and

Macdonald had got what they needed to make the movie on their own terms. It all seemed too good to be true.

"We sent them the script, told them Danny was director, no questions asked," said Macdonald. "They had no rights over casting and couldn't even see the film until we delivered it to them."

When they went to America to start pre-production in July 1996, McGregor was still in Ireland making *The Serpent's Kiss*. Initially, Macdonald's Figment team considered North Carolina for the shoot, but the weather was "too foggy" during their visit. They interpreted it as a bad omen, and opted instead for the vast expanses of Utah in the Mid-West. Boyle, a stickler for research, then went on a 10-day drive to get a feel for the area.

Casting was less problematic. Hodge had written the lead role specifically with Ewan McGregor in mind. Initially there was talk of casting Brad Pitt, but although he met Boyle and Macdonald, the latter insisted later that there was only ever one man for the job. The next question to arise was whether McGregor's character should be American or Scottish. After seeing the rushes from *Nightwatch*, in which he played an American, they decided McGregor was better sticking to his native accent. This turned out be a good decision. When *Nightwatch* opened in America in April 1998, McGregor's American accent was not well received by the critics. According to Mick LaSalle of the *San Francisco Chronicle*, "McGregor's American accent wobbles in and out, but it's amusing to watch the British struggle with that for a change."

Other critics were less kind—one even commented that McGregor "had to use every ounce of his limited talent just trying to suppress his accent, and he did a terrible job of it."

Highly-respected actors like Ian Holm and Stanley Tucci also joined the cast, and even Sean Connery was offered a cameo role as God. Although he declined owing to scheduling commitments, Connery took the time to tell Macdonald how much he had enjoyed *Trainspotting*.

The most difficult role to cast was that of the film's leading female character, the young kidnap victim, Celine. Five of America's top young actresses were interviewed before Boyle sent the script to Cameron Diaz, who had made her unforgettable debut in *The Mask*. The following day she flew from Chicago to Los Angeles to meet the director.

"As soon as she walked into the room I knew she was right," said Boyle. "She was unlike any of the other actresses I had met; very natural, very fun-loving and with a great sense of humour. I knew she would get on with Ewan like a house on fire."

Boyle left Diaz, in order to speak to Macdonald and Hodge by phone. "We've got to offer it to her. Now!" he told them. They thought it was a gamble, but agreed. Boyle went back into the room and offered Diaz the part.

It turned out that Boyle was right about his new leading lady and his leading man. When McGregor and Diaz met at the first rehearsal, they hit it off immediately and within minutes were singing and dancing together. Later, they were left alone in Salt Lake City's Tower Theater for a special screening of the Clark Gable–Claudette Colbert comedy *It Happened One Night*—good research for a film where Diaz wore the trousers in the relationship, and McGregor issued ransom demands with "please" and "thank you" attached.

On screen, the chemistry between Diaz and McGregor was obvious, but off-screen their friendship was also very close. On the set, they shared a trailer separated by a partition down the middle. McGregor told how they often talked to each other in the morning sitting on their own loos on either side of the partition, or watched countless videos while waiting to be called for their scenes.

The British media began to speculate just how close the young Scotsman and his American co-star really were. Later, during the promotion of *A Life Less Ordinary*, McGregor's affection for Diaz seemed to know no bounds. Sometimes they appeared together for interviews. "Oh my God. She's just a fantastic woman, so brilliant," he told one interviewer. "I knew within about two seconds that we were going to have a great time. She's an incredible lady. It wouldn't have been as good a film with anyone else. They wanted a big name Hollywood actress and they picked the best."

"I didn't know the chemistry would be there between us, but it was, luckily," he said in another interview. "Because from day one, it was obvious that we were going to have a good time. And I think because we were having such a good time, you can see it on the screen. You can see in our eyes that we're genuinely enjoying each other's company. It heightens all the romance and it heightens all the fun scenes.

There were bits that couldn't go in the film because we couldn't stop laughing. She is a really brilliant woman and a lovely lady, Cameron."

According to interviewer Chris Heath, writing in the British movie magazine *Neon*, McGregor told him: "Let's talk about [the movie], so long as we can stress how fucking great Cameron Diaz is. She's the best."

Diaz was equally complimentary. "In the film I fall in love with Ewan's character," she said. "And you can see how any girl could fall for him in real life, too. I loved Ewan's Scottish accent. He has sex appeal and he is going places. The Americans have already started asking who he is and that's the first sign of fame. He is an amazing guy, but he is married."

Charles Gant, describing his meeting with the pair in *The Face*, wrote: "Within minutes they've turned into the equivalent of a young married couple, finishing off each other's sentences, gentle mockery, almost continuous laughter and low-level flirting (if it wasn't for Ewan and Cameron being so avowedly in love with their respective partners, I'd suspect something)."

Asked by another interviewer if there were any love scenes in the movie, McGregor replied with a "devilish grin": "There were a few in the original script but we didn't shoot them. We did them out of work time . . . we were practising."

According to insiders on the film, it was all part of the plan. "There's no better way to publicise a film than to make a big issue of the relationship between the leading man and woman," said one. "The press can't get enough of that sort of stuff. Look what happened in the sixties when Richard Burton and Elizabeth Taylor were on the set of *Cleopatra*. There may have been an entirely different scenario, but their relationship got worldwide attention. It was magnificent publicity for the film. With Ewan and Cameron being two of the hottest and most attractive properties around, the same kind of questions were bound to be asked about them. They became genuinely good friends, but never anything more than that. There was no harm, though, in the press playing on how close they were. It was a great way to get the film known."

Because of the lengthy three-month shoot, McGregor's wife and daughter joined him in Utah. Eve worked on the film as a designer, and the family stayed in a rented flat in Salt Lake City. Talking about how he reconciled his on-screen relationship with his private life, McGregor said: "It's very nice to kiss Cameron Diaz but it doesn't give me any concern about when I get home to my wife because it's work," before adding jokingly: "It's not work, of course, kissing Cameron, but I'd like to tell you that it is."

On the shoot a routine developed. He spent his evenings with his wife and daughter, while at the weekends the crew usually descended on a biker's bar called Spanky's, where they would shoot pool and get drunk. Ewan quickly discovered that the more alcohol he consumed, the better he became on the pool table.

"We'd all go out and get fucking plastered. . . . With this film we kind of became normal people," he said.

On one such occasion McGregor and Diaz sang karaoke in a "rednecks" bar without being recognised. And Boyle surpassed himself with his rendition of the Sid Vicious' version of *My Way*.

Hodge, however, could not join in the revelry—he was back in London working as a senior house officer at St George's Hospital in Tooting. "He feels a certain duty to give something back," said one friend. "He trained for years at the taxpayers' expense and reckons that favour should be returned." Hodge himself said that "being a doctor is more interesting than writing scripts. It must be my middle-class Scottish background. If you don't go into medicine, accountancy or law, you're still some kind of deviant. I suppose the idea is to seek security. And I still feel that."

On *A Life Less Ordinary* McGregor was once again enjoying the security of working with the Figment Films crew. With cameraman Brian Tufano, editor Masahiro Hirakubo, production designer Kave Quinn and costume designer Rachael Fleming again on board, it was like being part of a repertory company, and McGregor himself had become an integral part of the team. "He is something special," said Macdonald. "He'll soon get offers which could make, break or turn him into a big star. We're lucky to have him. Tell him to take two steps back, one to the side and do a back flip while singing, and he'll do it three times exactly right. He looks ordinary, but he's magic-looking on camera. No question, he's part of our core team. It's four of us now."

Ewan McGregor liked nothing more than working with

the trio, especially Boyle, with whom he had formed an extraordinary actor/director bond. Such was his trust in Boyle's talents, McGregor said he would happily work with no-one else for the rest of his life, even if he didn't think the script was up to scratch. He believed the team would possibly make an unsuccessful movie, but never a bad one. No-one pushed him like Boyle, no-one forced him to get under the skin of characters quite like him. "He's the best there is, that's it," said McGregor. "I've never felt happier working with anyone else. He drains your creative juices and makes you work. Every take you do there is something you have to think about. He knows exactly what he is after, and he is brave enough to let it all come out. We work with him before the crew ever comes in to set up the scene. I'm fed up being told where to stand, 'stand here, stand there.' I'm usually saying, 'how the fuck do you know I'm going to stand over there? I may stand over here.' But because it has been story-boarded, you haven't got that option. You're just kind of like a puppet. But with Danny you're used as an actor, an artist. By the end of the day you've done some good work."

"I would turn down any of these bloomin' multi-million pound things if it meant conflicting with something he wanted me to do," he told another interviewer.

"I don't know what it is about Danny Boyle," he said. "If we knew we would all be making films like that. There's something about him. Everyone in the crew and cast always wants to do their best for him. He only ever gets pissed off at himself."

Boyle was equally keen to continue working with McGregor. "Ewan's a mate," said Boyle. "He's also the best film actor in Britain at the moment. He's Daniel Day Lewis and Gary Oldman rolled into one."

"He has got that thing Tom Hanks has. He's like the guy next door. He has got that ordinariness. That is his nature. He doesn't try to represent himself without spots, and I don't think he is thinking about that. It is instinct. There is something quite naughty about Ewan as well. Very naughty."

McGregor wanted to be in every movie they made. However, he was under no illusions that the time would come when his friends would not require him for a project. For McGregor, that would be a bitter pill to swallow, but an acceptable one. "It's not understood that I'll do all their films," he said. "I think what's brilliant about them is their loyalty and their belief in the team. However, the film is all important and if I wasn't right for a part, I wouldn't be cast in it. I know that the film's more important than their loyalty towards me. And I respect that. That's the way it should be."

Macdonald, however, was in no hurry to throw away the advantages of the collaborative process, no doubt remembering the spectacular success his grandfather Emeric Pressburger and his partner Michael Powell had enjoyed with their joint ventures over many years. "How many has De Niro done with Scorsese? Or Mastroianni with Fellini? Danny and Ewan still have a way to go, haven't they?"

But after three months sharing a trailer with Diaz, working with his favourite director and looking out over the remarkable vastness of the Rocky Mountains, McGregor was fed up. Not with the team, but with the inhabitants of Salt Lake City and their conservative ways. "The weirdest fucking people I've ever met" was the actor's verdict on the Mormon inhabitants of the area. "They're out of control with that shit," he complained. He could not understand people whose extreme religious beliefs set them apart from everything and everyone who did not share their views.

To the people of Salt Lake City, McGregor was a symbol of reckless youth, and having fun was seen as a threat to their existence. "I've got a black woollen hat with 'Pervert' written on the front," he said. "It's the name of a clothing label. We were in the supermarket one day and it was so cold I stuck it on Clara's head. I couldn't figure out why I was getting death looks. Then I realised my baby was wearing a Pervert hat. People were looking at me as if I was Satan. So I made a point of wearing it every time we went there."

"I got fed up," he told another interviewer. "You know, I got carded for buying cigarettes everywhere I went. I was like: 'Oh come on. Could you guys just relax? I'm 26 years old.' 'Yeah but I have friends that are 16 who look just like you.' 'Well, I'm not your friend then.' "

In American publications, McGregor was less critical, describing Utah as "interesting". "I don't want to offend all the burghers of Salt Lake City, but it was just a funny place. Quite a conservative area, I think." His more extreme outbursts, though, were reported back, and the good citizens were duly offended.

During promotion for the film, McGregor backtracked, even joking that if he turned up there for the premiere he would probably be targeted by Utah militiamen. "I've been quoted as saying the most awful things about Utah," he said. "And I'm so embarrassed, because I said some flippant, rude things that suddenly came out in bold print. I called them fucking weird people. And how dare I, really? So I'm apologising to everyone. Because, in fact, they made us feel so welcome on the whole. We had a really nice time, there, and it's a beautiful, beautiful state. However, Salt Lake City is a rather strange town."

Before he returned to Britain at the end of 1996, the publicity machine behind McGregor was already working hard to capitalise on his growing stature in the States. After talks with executives at NBC, an important deal was struck. He was to guest star on America's most popular TV series, *ER*.

In London, he had already filmed an episode of the supernatural series *Tales From The Crypt* for the American cable operator HBO. The episode, *Cold War*, was directed by Andy Morahan, and in it McGregor plays Ford, an American whose girlfriend, played by Jane Horrocks, gets involved with another man who turns out to be a vampire. A fight ensues, before the vampire turns into a bat and flies off, leaving McGregor and Horrocks to pick up the pieces. McGregor's American accent was impressive, but the episode was only shown on subscription channels to limited audiences.

Appearing in the third season of *ER* was an entirely

different proposition. It would mean maximum exposure throughout the USA, on a show so popular NBC would later pay a staggering $8 million for each episode.

In *The Long Way Around*, hot-head Duncan (McGregor) and his accomplice James (Currie Graham) attempt to rob a convenience store on St Valentine's Day. But the non-violent heist goes dramatically wrong when the shopkeeper shoots James. Duncan panics, shoots the owner, and several customers are injured. He then takes everyone in the store hostage. One of the customers, Nurse Hathaway (Julianna Margulies), manages to win his trust during the siege that follows. But when the shopkeeper dies, Duncan flees from the shop, is shot by a policeman and dies on the operating table in the ER.

The show went out in America on February 13, 1997, and McGregor earned an Emmy nomination for Outstanding Guest Appearance on a Drama Series. He lost out to Pruitt Taylor on *Murder One*, but his performance was applauded by the critics.

McGregor was thrilled to be part of a show he was a great fan of. "I did *ER* because I really like *ER*," he said. "I got an opportunity to do one and I thought it would be a laugh to see myself in an episode with all the people I'm used to watching in it."

He was also somewhat star-struck on the set. "They are great people. They've been doing it for three years together, so they're all quite 'snippy' with each other, not nastily, but their humour is quite personal. George Clooney is a very funny guy. He never knows his lines. He writes his lines on the beds, you know he is always looking down? He's reading his lines."

McGregor's riveting performance in one of season three's most compelling episodes extended his profile far beyond the audience who had enjoyed *Trainspotting*. "It was a really shrewd move to put him in a show like *ER*," said Mike Fleming, a columnist on the Hollywood showbiz bible *Daily Variety*. "He made a great critical impression here with *Trainspotting*. And he made a great impression when he did the *ER* episode. It was smart to get on *ER* because it is the highest rated show on TV. It was a great showcase for him. He's a fine young actor and a lot of people saw that. I think he has definitely been established as a guy to watch."

When McGregor returned to London after three months away, he had worked for virtually two years without a proper holiday. He decided it was time to take a few months off to spend more time with his family. Unfortunately, it was just then that Clara was struck down by meningitis. This was a traumatic experience for the McGregor family, but the youngster battled back to health.

McGregor returned to work in March 1997, joining the cast of *Velvet Goldmine*, a movie celebrating the glam rock period of the 1970s, in which he was to play the part of a gay rock star. But on the first day of filming he received the phone call that was destined to change his life forever.

XVII

Iggy, Ziggy, and Obi-Ewan Kenobi

Cigarette smoke filled the air as Curt Wild paced nervously around the room. In his smudged eyeliner, skin-tight snake-skin trousers and platform boots he looked faintly ridiculous. Awaiting his first big scene, he lit another cigarette, went through his lines one more time and, every so often, flicked back the fringe of his long blonde wig with fingers whose pallor contrasted starkly with nails painted jet black.

Just then the silence was shattered by the insistent, inescapable ringing of his mobile phone.

In the moment it took to answer the phone, Curt Wild

ceased to exist as Ewan McGregor slipped out of character and took the call.

It was his agent Lindy King. He could barely make out what she was saying, but when he did, he could hardly believe it. McGregor had got the part of Obi-Wan Kenobi in the new *Star Wars* trilogy.

As he ended the call, standing there in his outrageous glam rock gear, the realisation slowly dawned that a childhood dream had been realised. He was going to be in *Star Wars*, just like Uncle Denis all those years ago. It was possibly the biggest news of his life, but he had been sworn to secrecy—he could tell no-one.

It was March 1997, and McGregor's first day on the set of the glam rock movie *Velvet Goldmine*, in which he plays a rock star loosely based on Lou Reed and Iggy Pop.

"I couldn't do anything because I was on set and I wasn't allowed to tell anyone," recalled McGregor. For the rest of the day he remained tight-lipped, wandering around with a huge grin on his face. "So I was walking about like that . . . and people were saying: 'Are you all right.' And I was like: 'Yeah, fine.' "

"It was quite a day, knowing I got it and not being able to tell anyone," he said with a smile. "It was hard."

The press had already been speculating for some time about his chances of playing Obi-Wan in the new *Star Wars* films, but McGregor was under oath not to reveal the truth for two months. In the meantime he had to put the news to the back of his mind and concentrate on his role in *Velvet Goldmine*.

Created by the renegade American independent writer/
director Todd Haynes, and with REM's Michael Stipe as
executive producer, the film focuses on the sexually ambivalent glam rock scene of the early 1970s. It tells the story of
Brian Slade, played by Jonathan Rhys-Myers, a fictional
Bowie-like rock star who fakes his own assassination in
an attempt to escape from his glam rock stage persona. A
British journalist, Arthur (Christian Bale), starts investiga-
ting Slade's meteoric rise and fall, and tracks down his wife
Mandy (Toni Collette). She tells him about Slade's infatua-
tion with American singer, Curt Wild, played by McGregor.

Velvet Goldmine—the title came from a David Bowie B-side
from 1973—was said to have been inspired by the relationship
between David Bowie and Iggy Pop, and by the atmosphere
of an era when rock stars, particularly in Britain, followed
Bowie's lead in experimenting with multiple identities.
Bowie's Ziggy Stardust character was the most celebrated
example of this trend, incorporating all the usual rock 'n' roll
elements of drugs and alcohol combined with a suggestion
of bisexuality. "What was so interesting about that time,"
said producer Christine Vachon, "was that not only was it
OK to [experiment] with gender, you had to in order to be
musically successful. When you see some old *Top of the Pops*
from that time, even bands like the Rolling Stones, who
weren't associated with glam rock, wore lipstick and feather
boas. The whole movement was fascinating. In the end, it
went as far as it could. It was almost too dangerous."

The two-month shoot started in London in March 1997,

and the subject matter allowed McGregor to sample once again the more extreme aspects of life he revelled in on screen, but shied away from in real life. On one occasion, the noise of a gay sex scene being filmed on a rooftop in King's Cross caused consternation in the street below.

"In that scene I come offstage and he's in the wings," said McGregor, "and I take him up on to this rooftop and we have sex. Christian and I are both straight guys and we tried not to make too big a deal about it, and we were actually giving it full legs, which was brilliant. But it was going on for a very long time, I thought, with nobody yelling 'Cut'. Like, 'God, I would never be going on this long with a girl,' for instance."

When McGregor "came", he expected the scene to be over. But no-one said anything. With him and Bale both facing away from the cameras, they continued. He reckoned he must have climaxed too early and continued even faster. "I kept going, kept going, kept going, and by this time we were going so quick there was hair flying around (makes moaning sounds). And people on the street were going: 'What the fuck's going on there.' Finally, I said, 'Well, I'm going to look,' because Christian couldn't figure it out either."

Pushing his long blonde wig away from his eyes, McGregor turned to the crew. He was met by a disturbing scene. "People were picking up the tracks, and cables and wires and they just never said 'Cut'. We were still fucking away, four minutes later, giving it our all and they hadn't bothered to stop us. Bastards."

McGregor's outrageous on-screen character also gave him the opportunity to play out some of his childhood rock 'n' roll fantasies. In his early years, the only thing that would have stopped him becoming an actor was becoming a rock star. He had learned to play the guitar, and always wanted to be in a band. Despite being an accomplished guitarist and drummer, schooldays spent thrashing about with painted hair in Scarlet Pride were about as far as he got. He busked as a student at Guildhall, but turned down the chance to do an album of fifties cover versions after securing his big break in *Lipstick On Your Collar*. It would have taken him into the nightmare world of "Jason Donovan land", he said.

In *Velvet Goldmine* McGregor mimes to Iggy Pop songs, and he watched videos of the extrovert singer in order to gain inspiration. Michael Stipe also spent time coaching him for some of the concert scenes. In one of these, shot in a field south of London, the actor was asked by Haynes to round off with a typically outlandish finale.

McGregor agreed that the scene required something extreme. In front of more than 200 extras, with his trousers round his ankles, he exposed his by now famous appendage for all to see, while shouting "Fuck off." It was, apparently, a truly memorable moment. "I was mad when I was doing it," he said. But in the midst of the chaos on stage, McGregor was sane enough to ask himself: "What the hell am I doing?"

"I watched a lot of Iggy Pop [on video]. He's like a small kid, thrashing around in sporadic bursts, not even in time with the music sometimes. It's like he has to let it all out.

Having experienced doing that in front of 200 extras, I know that's the key to his character."

McGregor was fascinated by the experience of being a rock star. "It's the idea of standing there in front of all those thousands of people. It's just you, it's your music, it's not about pretending to be someone else. I don't have the guts but I would love to know what that feels like. It's a fantasy, the rock 'n' roll lifestyle. But because I've got a kid, I'm married and I've got a house, I can't do all that stuff."

The director, Haynes, a veteran of controversial movies like *Poison* and *Safe*, also entered into the radical spirit of the era his film was trying to recapture. He grew his hair into a Ziggy Stardust style, and had it dyed bright red. "I wanted to know what it felt like to wear super-tight skinny little tops that reveal you in ways that haven't been fashionable for men for quite a while now. And it really is a different feeling, being on platform shoes. It's what women experience every day. It was weird."

Velvet Goldmine's cast included the cult cross-dressing British comedian Eddie Izzard as the manager of a band, and Brian Molko, lead singer of Placebo (the band who were at the forefront of a nineties revival of glam rock) as a member of the New York Dolls. The glam rock era and its music, however, didn't really appeal to McGregor. "It's really annoying music, but fashion-wise, you drive through Camden and there are people wearing more outrageously seventies clothes than we wear in this film. It's a huge statement to make, but I'm not into all that. It seems a bit sad to me."

McGregor's musical tastes are much more nineties—he has been a big fan of Oasis ever since he heard their first album. Following an appearance on *Saturday Night Live* in America, he went drinking with Liam and Noel, who live in the same part of north London. "I was like a schoolgirl, sitting in their dressing room, going 'Ooooh. Oasis.'" According to friends, they became mates.

McGregor left the *Goldmine* set to prepare for the new *Star Wars* movie. The film's casting director, Robin Gurland, had started work on the film in July 1995, and she invited McGregor for a chat early the following year. Her first impression was that the Scot was right for the part of Obi-Wan, although for almost a year she continued to explore other possibilities—including Kenneth Branagh. In the end, she returned to McGregor. "First instincts are usually best," she said. "This was true in the case of Ewan."

In early 1997, Gurland met McGregor again. Then he met with the film's creator George Lucas and the prequel producer Rick McCallum. One morning in March came the all-important screen test with Liam Neeson. The star of *Rob Roy* and *Schindler's List* was in the running for the part of the master Jedi who trains the young Kenobi in the ways of the Force, and Lucas and McCallum wanted to see if these two actors had that special master/student chemistry that would be so important on screen. It soon became clear that McGregor and Neeson had exactly what they were looking for.

It was a strange day for McGregor. He left the screen test

to attend the funeral of an actor friend, Ronald Fraser, whom he had known from his local pub, before going home to get ready for the British premiere of the reworked *Star Wars* original in London that evening.

A few days later, on the *Goldmine* set, came the call from Lindy King telling him he had the part. "It felt pretty amazing," said McGregor, who just couldn't keep the news to himself. "I told my wife, because 'fuck them, I'm telling my wife', and my parents, and that was it. I didn't tell anyone else for a long while."

McGregor had never had much interest in Hollywood blockbusters, but, paradoxically, he did not see *Star Wars* in quite the same light. This was something different, something unique, but—rather like his talent—the difference was some-how indefinable. Perhaps it all went back to his childhood in Crieff, seeing his uncle Denis Lawson flashing across the screen in the original *Star Wars* movies. Now, it seemed likely his own daughter Clara would experience the new trilogy at roughly the same age he experienced the originals.

McGregor himself was just a toddler when a young film-maker called George Lucas first started work on his ground-breaking intergalactic epic. In many ways, Lucas was just like McGregor. Raised in a small town in California, the ironically named Modesto, his fascination with films came from the black and white images he immersed himself in as a boy growing up in the 1950s.

Lucas rose from the obscurity of Modesto to study film-making at the University of Southern California, before emerging from the shadow of directors like Francis Ford Coppolla to make his own movies. After a false start with his first feature, the poorly received *THX 1138*, a dark sci-fi tale, he achieved notable success in 1973 with *American Graffiti*. Initially shown at only two cinemas in LA and New York, this semi-autobiographical look at the years of Lucas' youth quickly gained a huge cult following. Its story of teenage angst set against a soundtrack of early sixties hits ensured its widespread appeal. Described as a "classic sleeper", *Graffiti* went on to open across the country, and was still showing at some cinemas more than a year later. It was made for just $750,000, but eventually earned a staggering $117 million at the worldwide box office. It was a "wonder film" that provided the incentive for sceptical executives at 20th Century Fox to fund his next project—*Star Wars*.

Lucas had harboured ambitions of writing his space fantasy for years, and finally began work in April 1973. His original storyline was influenced by classic fairytales, mythology, and even old TV shows like *Captain Blood* and *Flash Gordon*. His first draft, however, *The Story of Mace Windu*, was very different from the epic adventure that would finally reach the screen. At one point a 12-year-old Princess Leia was the central character, but she was soon replaced by the rebellious Luke Starkiller. Only on the first day of filming was his name changed to Skywalker. The title went through almost as many changes as the screenplay, from *The Adventures of the Starkiller, Episode One of the Star Wars* to the eventual *Star Wars*. Two Hollywood studios, Universal and United Artists, rejected

Lucas' script, before an executive at 20th Century Fox, Alan Ladd Jnr, recognised its potential.

The production was massive, with a budget that eventually spiralled to more than $10 million—a huge figure for 1976. It was filmed at Elstree Studios in England, and on location in Tunisia, before post-production began in LA. Perhaps the most extraordinary aspect of the film's production was that it depended for its success on ground-breaking special effects—effects which Lucas demanded, but which were far more ambitious than anything that had been done before.

The cast, led by Mark Hamill and Carrie Fisher, were largely unknown. One of the supporting actors in *Graffiti*, who had returned to a successful career as a carpenter, was also brought in—his name was Harrison Ford. The film's only established star was the highly-respected British actor Alec Guinness, in the role of Obi-Wan Kenobi. British composer John Williams was enlisted to produce the score.

When *Star Wars* was released on May 25, 1977, the industry was predicting an expensive disaster. Although the film was initially only shown in selected cinemas, the sceptics were soon confounded, as *Star Wars* went on to break box-office records across America, becoming the most successful movie of all time and pulling in more than $400 million worldwide. In San Francisco the number of people who saw the film exceeded the city's 750,000 population.

The Empire Strikes Back followed in 1980, and three years later came *Return of the Jedi*. The trilogy was hailed as one of the most significant movie events of recent times. It marked a revolution in film-making—the special effects were light years ahead of their time and, perhaps more importantly, *Star Wars* was the first movie that fully exploited spin-off merchandising. After *Return of the Jedi*, the series had generated sales worth billions of dollars. Its critics even suggested that *Jedi* was just an advertising vehicle for the seemingly endless stream of toys, games and other merchandising opportunities that followed relentlessly in its wake.

From the very outset, Lucas negotiated sequel, musical soundtrack, and merchandising rights in exchange for lower fees. It was a masterstroke from a man whose vision was not confined to the screen. At the time, Fox thought they had struck a good deal, but soon came to regret it as one of the biggest mistakes in movie history. One of the most enduring legacies of *Star Wars* was that Hollywood made sure this never happened again.

In 1994, *Daily Variety* broke the story that Lucas was returning to the *Wars*. Persistent rumours that he was writing three prequels turned out to be true. He had been persuaded the new trilogy was possible after seeing what Steven Spielberg achieved with the remarkable special effects that helped *Jurassic Park* surpass many of the records *Star Wars* had set. He also made public his intention to return to directing for the first prequel.

The enthusiastic reaction to his announcement was perhaps not surprising. The pull of *Star Wars* had never waned—there were thousands of fan clubs, and conventions regularly took place in every corner of the globe. Books, comics and radio shows were produced on each individual aspect of the movie.

In 1996 and 1997 the original trilogy was revamped with new special effects and re-released around the world to commemorate the 20th anniversary. Once again it packed out cinemas, and earned hundreds of millions of dollars. Fathers who had been boys the first time round took their kids to see the updated versions, and *Star Wars* won a whole new army of fans. In America all three films made the list of the year's top 10 movies. Special video boxed sets later broke yet more records.

For those involved in the making of *Star Wars*, the effects were far-reaching—although not always beneficial. Lucas withdrew from the Hollywood studio system, and blamed the movies for the break-up of his marriage. Gary Kurtz, the producer on the original, was made bankrupt in 1986. Carrie Fisher's life descended into a drugs hell after the trilogy. And Mark Hamill couldn't get work on anything else. He felt as if he had "copyright Lucasfilm stamped on my ass". Meanwhile, Harrison Ford quietly became one of the biggest movie stars in the world.

When Ewan McGregor accepted the role of Obi-Wan Kenobi in March 1997 he was becoming part of a project far bigger than the originals had been. Although the budget for the first prequel was only around £40 million—relatively small by today's standards—the money surrounding the film was mind-boggling. In May 1996 Pepsi beat off a string of huge bids to associate itself with the new trilogy, winning the contract to use McGregor's and other characters' images on its products and those of subsidiaries like Pizza Hut and Kentucky Fried Chicken. The amount paid for the privilege was an unprecedented $2 billion.

The following year two American companies struck the biggest ever toy licensing agreement to produce an assortment of toys for the new movies. Ewan McGregor action figures would feature alongside many others.

Star Wars had become bigger than any of the blockbusters with which McGregor had said he would never become involved. But had he ever considered refusing the part of Obi-Wan?

"I don't really like big blockbuster films and the LA studio thing," he said. "I've been quite vocal about that. And then people say: 'But you're doing *Star Wars*?' And I do see [it] as a different kind of thing . . . something unique. Of course you have to do them if they ask you. You can't turn it down. If they ask you: 'Do you want to be Obi-Wan Kenobi?' you just cannot say no."

As he told one interviewer: "When you're my age, and you were out there cheering when the first *Star Wars* came out, what are you going to do when they offer one of the leads in the new film? Say no? No way. Can you imagine what it'll be like sitting down in some screening room, the curtain goes up and there it is, the new movie? Magic."

XVIII

1997: A Space Odyssey

As the battle raged all around him, he couldn't take his eyes off the immense bulk of the Death Star, hurtling towards him at incredible speed. Struggling to control his X-wing fighter as it passed through the storm of enemy fire coming in from all sides, Wedge Antilles felt the tremendous shock wave as his craft was hit. . . .

Meanwhile, in a small cinema in a galaxy far, far away Denis Lawson sat watching the first preview performance of *Star Wars*. He was watching himself—or at least his alter-ego Wedge—on screen, but was puzzled that Wedge's voice seemed to belong to someone else. Lawson smiled. Surely his American accent couldn't have been that bad? But at that moment he couldn't care less. The movie was fantastic, he was in it, voice or no voice, and as far as he was concerned it wasn't likely to be one of the more significant roles of his career.

As Lawson walked through the cinema foyer afterwards, he spotted a concerned-looking Mark Hamill coming towards him.

"Denis, they've revoiced you," he said.

No doubt Lawson appreciated Luke Skywalker's sympathy, but he was mature enough to realise how the system worked. "Oh yeah, I was really heartbroken," joked the actor years later.

The incident summed up Lawson's ambivalent attitude towards being part of the greatest screen trilogy of all time. His character, the glorified extra Wedge, was the only character apart from the main cast to survive all three films. But in a world where people discussed the exact type of Yak's hair used to make Chewbacca's costume, and debated the viability of the futuristic technology of the Death Star, Denis Lawson became an improbable cult hero for the seemingly limitless number of dedicated fans. Novels were written about his character, and in the nineties the rise of the internet led to websites devoted specifically to him.

Incredibly, there was even speculation speeding around the superhighway that he was dead—because of a simple spelling mistake in the credits. In the first two movies, his name was spelt D-e-n-n-i-s Lawson. By *Return of the Jedi*, the "error" had been rectified and he became D-e-n-i-s. But some fans suspected a conspiracy, believing Lawson had died and been replaced by an actor with an almost identical name for the final episode.

Lawson, who even received letters on the subject, reacted with bemusement. "There was a theory apparently that I hadn't been available so they had shot it with someone else on a secret sound stage. I wrote back to this guy and said basically: 'Why are you wasting your time on this drivel?'"

Ironically, Lawson's birth certificate records his first name as Dennis, with two n's. Carol McGregor always thought it was with one n, and according to Lawson's agent, so did he. He has always spelt it Denis. It seemed the people at *Star Wars* were not the only ones who were confused.

On another occasion he was in a cafe in Philadelphia with an American actor who informed the two young barmen they were serving Wedge from *Star Wars*. "They just freaked," said Lawson. "I said all I did was fly around and one of them said: 'No man, you changed my life.' I find it very puzzling."

The bit-parts in the trilogy were just fleeting episodes in an impressive cinema, TV and stage career, but the fan-mail from *Star Wars* still outweighed everything else. It was a source of annoyance to an actor who came to regard the films as something of a millstone round his neck.

"They are fantastic films and they are a huge part of cinema culture," he said. "As an acting job, for me they were virtually non-existent, almost one of the most insignificant jobs I have ever done. And the fact I get more fan-mail for that than anything else is slightly irritating. It is odd, but at the same time it doesn't actually mean very much to me. Honestly, those jobs didn't. Ewan's work in the films they've just shot is a major, meaty and enjoyable role. But mine wasn't. So the connection for me is really tenuous. For a lot of people it's: 'Oh, you were there and now he's there. Oh my God.' It doesn't mean diddly shit to me."

After studying drama in Glasgow in the sixties, Lawson cut his teeth for several years on the Scottish repertory theatre circuit. It was a tough period that produced a lot of sweat and tears, but little money. In the mid-1970s he moved to London, where he quickly built up an impressive reputation in TV, film and on the stage. Aside from *Star Wars*, he is probably best known for his role as the hotel owner in Bill Forsyth's *Local Hero*, alongside Burt Lancaster. Lawson also won acclaim in the drama *Dead Head*, the BBC comedy series *The Kit Curran Radio Show*, and later as a maverick lawyer in the BBC drama, *The Justice Game*, a role regarded by some as his finest. Most recently, he starred in the BBC series *The Ambassador*. His stage work included the raunchy *Lust*, and Ewan McGregor's particular favourites—the 1980 performance of *Pal Joey*, and *50 Words—Bits of Lenny Bruce*. Coached by Lawson, McGregor used extracts from the latter for his college speeches.

Lawson acted as mentor to his nephew in his early acting career, and was also close to Ewan's brother Colin. The youngsters went to see him in everything he did. These days they are close friends who drink together, jam on their guitars together and confide in each other.

"Denis helped me with my audition speeches when I started out," said McGregor. "He has always been there for me to give advice. His success is partly why I am here. Denis feels a bit silly being associated with *Star Wars*. He's done so many other things but many people know him for that."

Lawson spotted McGregor's potential early on at drama college, where he stood out from the rest of the class. "Ewan is a different personality to me and I think one of the reasons he succeeds is because he is very self assured and has a very strong sense of who he is, which he is able to project. It usually takes actors a few years to find that and he had it right from the word go. When he was thinking of training, I advised him, but I'm not some kind of guru. Ewan absolutely has made his own decisions and knows how to work for himself. And boy does he work."

Lawson admitted that he thought the idea of both of them being in *Star Wars* was a bit spooky: "a little bit odd for me, really". When shooting started on the first prequel, at Millennium Studios in Leavesden, Hertfordshire in June 1997, Lawson joined McGregor and Lucas for lunch on the set. In the canteen there were the inevitable cries of "Wedge!".

"He came up and sat with me," said McGregor. "And he met George, and he said: 'George, you're still wearing the same shirt.' And he was, apparently."

It may still have been the same shirt, but Lucas' attention to detail meant nothing was left to chance in his work. He had started work on the *Star Wars* prequels more than three years before principal photography began.

The decision to film in Britain was taken primarily because of the lower costs involved, but even so the fee paid by the studio for the use of the former Rolls Royce site was rumoured to be easily the biggest in British movie history.

Construction workers spent months building more than 50 sets inside the old hangars, only for them to be taken down a few days later when filming was completed. The crew numbered more than 600, a figure comparable to that in any of the biggest blockbusters. Security, however, was far tighter than usual. Barbed wire fencing was erected all around the site, and a security checkpoint set up at the main gate. Everyone from McGregor downwards was required to sign a confidentiality contract, agreeing not to speak about the casting or production.

A computerised photo ID swipe card was needed to get on to the set and access was restricted to individual stages, while security guards kept people away from sensitive areas. "It was the most secretive operation I've ever seen," said one construction worker. "The James Bond movie *Goldeneye* was filmed there and that was so easy-going by comparison. This time you weren't allowed to stray away from your own area. The guards didn't smile at all."

Although unusual elsewhere, such extraordinary levels of secrecy were commonplace on Lucas sets. *The Empire Strikes Back's* most dramatic plot twist came when Darth Vader told Luke Skywalker he was his father. But on set, the 6' 7" actor inside Vader's outfit played out a completely different storyline. Englishman David Prowse only discovered the real truth when the voice of James Earl Jones revealed all at the American premiere. During the making of *Return of the Jedi,* when Skywalker told Princess Leia he was her brother, the crew, and even the sound man, were asked not to listen.

Inevitably, the plot of the prequels became the subject of intense speculation, particularly on the internet. Production supervisor David Brown said no decoy scenes were produced this time around, but still insisted that secrecy was vital if cinema-goers were to get value for money. "We wrap it all up with confidentiality because it is necessary," he said. "People's expectations are very high. Who wants to see a film like *Star Wars* when they know all about the characters and the story before they go in?"

In another unprecedented move, the *Star Wars* prequel was the first movie to have a 24-hour production schedule. After filming in Europe, Lucas sent the rushes by satellite to the USA for the special effects wizards at ILM in Los Angeles to work on overnight.

Filming moved to Naples on July 22, and for five days the cast shot scenes in La Reggia di Caserta, a stunning local museum, before moving on to the same area of Tunisia where much of the original was shot.

But, just a few days into shooting, disaster struck. A massive desert storm swept through the huge set that had taken months to assemble. Torrential rain, sand and winds of up to 100 m.p.h. wreaked havoc, and left a scene of utter devastation. Articulated trucks were tossed into the air like toys, props weighing as much as two tonnes were thrown

100 yards, and the three huge marquees housing the costumes, props and make-up facilities were flattened. The actors' tents were also blown away.

"It was a very, very big storm," said David Brown, "and the centre of it hit our set. Back in the town where we were staying I was aware of the storm hitting about eight in the evening. So we pulled some people together and went out in a couple of four wheel drives about half two the next morning to see what it was like. It was a dirt road out from the town and we wanted to see if we could get there because the road may have been taken out."

Brown was not prepared for the scene that greeted him when he finally arrived. "It was just devastation," he said. "I went away and had a quick cry, then came back and got on with it. We had been in preparation there for five months and it was a real achievement to get it together. To see that level of devastation in such a short time had an enormous impact on everyone."

The crew feared the worst. They were scheduled to be in Tunisia for three weeks but suddenly those plans looked doomed. The following morning a huge effort was mounted to salvage the set. Dozens of construction workers were flown in from Britain, and three hundred extras were given new jobs as salvage operators. According to Brown, everyone rolled up their sleeves to save the production.

Amazingly, filming started again at 11 o'clock that morning, just four hours behind schedule. Even the worst affected sets were back in use within five days. "The impact was staggering but we recovered very quickly," added Brown. "For me, that was the real achievement."

After three and a half weeks filming in Tunisia, the crew returned to Britain to complete the 14-week shoot. For Ewan McGregor and the rest of the cast there had been a lot of hanging around. Although they had been in Tunisia for almost a month, they had actually filmed for only 12 days.

But as far as McGregor was concerned, the boredom didn't really matter. He was too caught up in the atmosphere of *Star Wars*. McGregor felt the characters were almost like members of his own family, and the first time he saw R2D2 he instinctively went to bow down on the ground. "I walked into the props room and there were about 50 props makers, all of them guys, and I saw R2D2 at the end of the room. I just started going: 'Aaaaaaaaa.' All the props makers turned round and they all knew how I felt."

McGregor experienced similar feelings of nostalgia the first time he was presented with a box of light-sabre handles and asked to choose a colour. On the first day of rehearsals the crew burst into laughter as he went through a fight scene.

"Ewan was doing the noises that the light-sabre makes," said a friend. "Maybe it was what he did as a kid, maybe it was just natural but everyone just laughed their heads off. Ewan says he always felt like he should do the noises himself anyway."

The light-sabres were also "bloody lethal" according to McGregor. On one occasion he burnt his hands on one, and hit a technician on the head when he threw it to the side.

"There's nothing cooler than being a Jedi Knight," he said. "It's so familiar wearing all the Jedi stuff, the clogs and the light-sabres. And I'm actually like: 'What is this?' It's part of your childhood, and you're involved in it. It's very weird.

"The first day I got dressed properly it was quite a moment for a boy from Scotland to stand there and look in the mirror: 'Jedi McGregor'."

Star Wars was unlike anything McGregor had ever experienced before. It was the biggest film he had worked on, but also the most restrictive. With directors like Danny Boyle, he was able to make suggestions and improvise. Often, he was encouraged to do so. But with Lucas the actors were only a tiny part of the equation. In the great scheme of things the actual shoot was minute in comparison to the planned 18 months of post-production, when the all-important special effects would be added. Only two of the 50 sets at Leavesden were complete—the rest would have their virtual backgrounds and effects inserted back in Los Angeles. As a result, McGregor did much of his work against "bluescreen", the blank canvas upon which the special effects wizards would work their magic.

Although the actor found this tightly structured approach utterly frustrating, he understood the need for it. And despite the fact that the shoot was incredibly hard work, he loved it—even though the script did little to stretch his acting talents. He joked about the limits of the dialogue, recalling how there was a lot of fighting and frowning—and not much else. How many different kinds of frown could he adopt for the camera, he wondered. Sometimes, it felt like he was starting out again.

"There are 18 months of post-production, two years of pre-production and three and a half months of shooting," he said. "That shows you how important the acting is. But I never walked into it expecting to give an Oscar-winning performance. I think I did a good job and the film will come out to be absolutely what it was meant to be."

It was a matter of "just getting down to it," he said. "What am I going to say? George, your dialogue's crap."

"It was so, so complex with the special effects and stuff. You were just hanging around for days and days."

For McGregor, the wonder of *Star Wars* would not be in the making, but in seeing himself in the completed film. "The exciting thing will be seeing it in the preview theatre," he said. "Watching it and seeing what they've put round about you. What wasn't there is suddenly there."

The film, rumoured to be entitled *The Balance Of The Force* was scheduled to be released in American cinemas on May 25, 1999, known as Lucas Day following the successes of the first trilogy. The prequels revolve around the rise of the Empire and the downfall of Anakin Skywalker, who eventually crosses to the dark side of the Force to become Darth Vader. The exact details of the plot are still shrouded in secrecy, but in the first movie the future Emperor Palatine (Ian McDiarmid) is thought to be trying to overthrow the old Republic. Obi-Wan Kenobi (McGregor) and Neeson's mystic warrior are the only surviving Jedis after their order is ruthlessly exterminated by Boba Flett and his Mandalorian warriors. They flee to the desert city of Tatooine, while Palatine embraces the dark side of the Force. He realises the Jedi are a threat to his side of the Force and sends a legion of storm-troopers to crush them. They flee to an underwater city where the final battle takes place.

"It is amazing," said David Brown. "It is a big piece of cinema history. This time round George has gone out of his way to make sure there is a strong cast and he has got it. He just wanted the best people for the job. But even though it is a very strong cast, it is not a Hollywood cast. It is a cast for the picture. In this case, the film is the star. George is making a film which is really heralding a new period in cinema. We have fully realised not just computer animated characters, but humanoid characters. . . . You no longer have a situation where you have to dress up a character in a woolly suit. You can now build both practical and virtual sets that will defy imagination."

Brown was deeply impressed by McGregor's performance in the film. "I think Ewan and everyone else had a lot of fun," he said. "He was right for the part. I think it worked absolutely perfectly, the relationship between him and Liam Neeson as the older Jedi, the Jedi Master. There was a master-pupil relationship there which was important. There's no question that Ewan is the best person out there, not just as the young Obi-Wan Kenobi. We were not trying to find a young Alec Guinness, we were trying to find a young Obi-Wan. Ewan was the best for that role. And there was no question that people really wanted to come and work on this movie. Samuel L. Jackson was in the film because he wanted to be in it."

Although in acting terms the role of Obi-Wan Kenobi threw up few challenges for McGregor, he was slightly apprehensive about following in Alec Guinness' footsteps. "Sir Alec has done some of the most incredible cinematic acting I have ever seen," said Ewan, "and yet he is a legend for playing Obi-Wan Kenobi in half of a *Star Wars* movie. To be remembered just as Obi-Wan must be very weird. I think he is still really confused about it himself."

Despite this, McGregor insisted he was never intimidated by the prospect of taking on such a major role.

"I've played harder parts," he said. "Alec Guinness was asked about acting in *Star Wars* and he said: 'There is not a lot of psychological racking around to do here. Deliver the lines and hope the background is nicely lit.' It's not demanding in terms of emotions, but it was very tiring because of the slow process with the special effects. Sci-fi movies are really tough. It's lots of bluescreen, and George Lucas comes in and says: 'OK, you're in a space ship and you start it up.' Vrrooooom, vrrooooom. We'd laugh, because you have to use your imagination completely."

XIX

REBEL WITHOUT A PAUSE

When Ewan McGregor left the set of *Star Wars* late that September his image was everywhere. Anyone walking into a British newsagent's was met by a wall of pictures of the hottest actor around. Women's, youth culture and film magazines couldn't get enough of him. Neither could the newspapers. He seemed to be on every cover. As he commented later: "you can't deny it's quite nice seeing yourself. When you're walking past the newsagent's: 'That's me, that's me.' I quite like that."

The timing of this publicity barrage could hardly have been more favourable. The eagerly anticipated *A Life Less Ordinary* was due out on October 24 on both sides of the

Atlantic, and the film's PR machine was doing everything possible to make it a success.

They wanted maximum publicity, and would have no trouble getting it. It seemed that Boyle, Macdonald and Hodge could do no wrong, while McGregor was already Britain's top film star, and had just finished making one of the most hyped movies of recent times. The glamour of Cameron Diaz—spiced up with a heady cocktail of rumour and innuendo—was merely the icing on the cake.

During the *Star Wars* shoot, McGregor had given interviews to journalists from key magazines, and as the whole team set off on an extensive promotional tour of North America and Europe, maximum exposure was more or less guaranteed. Indeed, the film would become easily the most hyped in Britain that year.

In America, the premiere was a star-studded affair with two of McGregor's idols, Noel Gallagher and Debbie Harry, attending. "There is this scene when I'm crossing the street bringing Cameron groceries, and I'm actually singing one of Oasis' B-sides (a song called *Round Our Way*)," said McGregor. "And I was so embarrassed knowing Noel was there. He said he was going to stand up and boo, but he didn't."

Trainspotting took more than $60 million worldwide, but it was hoped that figure would be exceeded by *A Life Less Ordinary*. The critics, however, were less than impressed.

"What a title, the best of year, without a doubt," wrote Tom Shone in *The Sunday Times*. "Beyond that, however, and the movie goes to pieces, although I'm still working on the theory that if you were able to take the amount of drugs consumed by Ewan McGregor in *Trainspotting*, the whole thing would make perfect sense."

If Boyle had been attempting to take on the Americans on their own soil, he had fallen flat on his face, Shone concluded. *The Independent on Sunday's* Matthew Sweet believed the film failed by concentrating too much on wacky embellishments, and not enough on plot. "This is muddle in the guise of marvel, and screwball comedy doesn't tolerate such lackadaisical treatment. It requires razor-sharp plotting and a passionate attachment to logic. Neither are forthcoming." And despite all the hype, movie fans voted with their feet and stayed away in droves. In Britain gross takings amounted to just £3.4 million—almost two million less than *Shallow Grave*, while in America the film took a meagre $4.3 million at the box office. *A Life Less Ordinary* had bombed. The American magazine *Entertainment* voted it the third biggest flop of the year, behind *The Saint* and *Speed 2*.

"Given the expectations and hype it was a bit of a disaster," said one film industry insider. "It wasn't a bad film but people compared it with *Trainspotting*, which was really a modern classic. I think if the guys were guilty of anything, it was of trying too hard. There was maybe too much going on, and ultimately the film as a whole didn't work. This will not affect their standing, though. They will hopefully learn from the experience and come back stronger."

McGregor launched a stout defence against the film's poor

reception. "I think it was inevitable that no matter what sort of film these guys made, they were in for a backlash. How do you follow up a movie like *Trainspotting*? To try and make *Trainspotting Part 2* would have been ridiculous, so I think they did completely the right thing and just went off in a completely different direction."

But there was little time to dwell on the movie's poor performance, as McGregor's packed schedule took him to the seaside town of Scarborough in the north-east of England at the end of October to begin filming *The Rise and Fall of Little Voice*.

Based on a play by Jim Cartwright, the film was a long-cherished project of his friend, *Brassed Off* director Mark Herman's, and McGregor's decision to commit himself more than a year earlier had helped secure funding from Miramax in America. Although the nine-week shoot was due to run until December 20, all McGregor's scenes were to be shot by mid-November.

Little Voice had a star-studded cast, including Michael Caine, Brenda Blethyn, Jim Broadbent and Jane Horrocks—who had played the lead role in the original West End stage version. But there were to be no Hollywood-style pay cheques —the main cast members all agreed to take an equal cut.

The film is a kind of a modern-day version of the Cinderella story, set in a British seaside town. Horrocks plays Little Voice, a shy woman who finds a soul-mate in telephone engineer Billy, played by McGregor. Although she is painfully shy, her singing voice is magnificent. When a seedy small-time agent Ray Say (Caine) discovers her, he believes he has found his ticket out of obscurity and sells everything to make his dream come true. Triumph and tragedy quickly follow.

Even in the short time he spent on set, McGregor made a big impression. "Ewan was brilliant," said producer Elisabeth Karlsen. "He is a great actor and we loved making the film with him."

But as usual McGregor had no time to rest. He finished *Little Voice* at midnight on Sunday, November 17, and was on the set of his next movie, *Rogue Trader*, at Pinewood Studios, just nine hours later. He was clearly a man in demand, but friends felt he was taking too much on, and some told him to start taking time out.

"He got to the stage where a film would possibly only get the go ahead if he committed to it," said one friend. "So if he really liked the script that was it. There was no going back. He's not a moralistic person by any means but if he says he will do something, he will do it. Everyone else works 45 to 50 weeks of the year so he doesn't really understand why it should be different for an actor."

Rogue Trader tells the story of Nick Leeson, the financial whizz-kid blamed for the crash of Barings—one of the world's oldest merchant banks. As general manager at the Singapore office, he wheeled and dealed on the world's markets, moving millions of pounds every day. But he also manipulated the bank's balances to hide massive losses. As a result, Barings collapsed with debts of $800 million and Leeson went to jail.

The film is an adaptation of Leeson's autobiography, with a screenplay by James Dearden, who had previously written *Fatal Attraction*. Dearden, who also directed, concentrated on Leeson's working-class roots and his unlikely rise to prominence in the world of merchant banking. Those in charge of Barings emerge particularly badly from the script, and the film's executive producer, David Frost, suggested that Leeson would never have gone to jail had he come from an upper-class background.

This only served to polarise opinion about what was always going to be a controversial film. Some people in the City were angry it was being made at all, while many others were irate that Leeson, a convicted criminal, was apparently going to profit from his crime. The film's producers argued that any money Leeson made would be swallowed up by legal fees, but this did little to quieten the controversy by the time the production moved to Malaysia and Singapore in early 1998.

McGregor wore one of Leeson's Gucci ties in the film— apparently Leeson never made a penny while wearing it—but did not visit Leeson in jail, although he said he might meet him when he got out sometime around 2000. "I would have been embarrassed," McGregor said. "What would I say? Hi, I'm playing you in a movie, and you're rotting in jail.' It would be awful."

Asked for his personal views on Leeson, McGregor told another interviewer: "I don't want to have any opinion about him . . . because people are very black and white about the case. Some people think he's a complete animal and some people think he's a victim. I want to play it in the middle."

Anna Friel, best known for her role in the British TV soap *Brookside,* and her appearance in the recent BBC adaptation of Dickens' *Our Mutual Friend,* plays Leeson's wife in the film. She felt that the similarities between herself and McGregor contributed to their on-screen performance: "We are male and female versions of each other. His parents are both teachers; so are mine. His brother flies for the RAF; so does mine. We both have two fingers up to the class thing and the American thing. . . . Because of all that, we've given a great performance together." Off screen, McGregor and Friel became friends, as she told *The List* in March 1998: "Ewan is the best, he is a wonderful guy."

For the film's star, however, trouble was lurking just around the corner when photos of him kissing his co-star appeared in tabloid newspapers back home. Inevitably, there was even speculation that they were having an affair. But the real story was far less sordid than the picture painted by the tabloids. Some of the photographs were taken during filming—Friel was after all playing Leeson's wife—while others simply captured an innocent greeting between two friends.

McGregor and Friel, however, were furious with the press. Friel suggested that some sections of the media chose to ignore the fact that the pair were simply "soul mates" because speculation about something more serious was more titillating for their readers. Like many before her, she was exasperated by the behaviour of the tabloids, and her final word on the matter was: "Let them think what they want."

"It was the first time anything like that had happened to Ewan and he was disgusted by it," said a friend. "It didn't cause any trouble with Eve because their relationship is built on great trust. They are totally wrapped up in each other. But it made him even more suspicious about some of the newspapers."

When McGregor returned home at the end of January he was physically and mentally drained. It had been a good year, but the heavy workload of the previous ten months had taken its toll. He seemed only to see Clara when she was sleeping, and decided he had to find more time between films. A month off in February seemed like a good start.

"One thing he has learned is to try and take a little time off between shoots," said a friend. "There were only a matter of hours between finishing *Little Voice* and starting *Rogue Trader*. And although he loves the fact he is always learning when doing films, he learned on that occasion never to do that again. He doesn't think he overworks necessarily, but he knew that was too quick a change."

According to Denis Lawson, the trait runs in the family— after all, in 1998 Ewan's gran, Phyllis, was still running her shop back in Crieff at the age of 75. "She is a human dynamo," said Lawson in February that year. "Our family are always on the go. Last year Ewan probably overworked. But he is planning to slow himself up. I would be interested to see if he can do it, though."

McGregor himself insisted he was getting better at dealing with spare time, but conceded: "I'm still fractious when I get a bit of time on my hands, I get all fidgety."

"I really should take a holiday, I know," he told another interviewer in late 1997, "but for me there is nothing better than arriving on a film set in the morning and just being someone new. I'm sure I'll be able to work all this out with a therapist in later years, but for now, making movies is just too much fun to stop and think about it."

He had been working almost continuously since the *Shallow Grave* shoot more than four years earlier. He had recorded voice-overs, including one for Virgin Atlantic, and had followed in the footsteps of stars like Sean Connery and Jodie Foster, filming adverts for Japanese television. One was for Bobson denims and the other for Beatnik, a soft drink. These short commercials reputedly netted him around £200,000 each.

In general, however, McGregor shied away from the limelight. He had no interest in self-promotion—especially on television, claiming that when De Niro did *Letterman* so would he. It was not until 1996 that he gave his first big interview on British TV, appearing on Chris Evans' *TFI Friday*. And even then he got himself into trouble. During the interview, McGregor said "fuck", and although he apologised immediately, the programme-makers were given a stiff warning by TV watchdogs. Jim McGregor even asked Ewan to tone down his swearing in interviews because it embarrassed the conservative citizens of Crieff. In January 1998, McGregor was still reluctant to appear on TV—he did not want to go on Michael Parkinson's reborn chat show, until his mother, who was a big fan of the programme, persuaded him to appear.

His other TV appearances have included dressing up as Minnie Mouse for an Elton John show; presenting Oasis with an MTV music award; and, along with Cameron Diaz, announcing the winner of the Best Kiss at the MTV movie awards, an experience that left him unimpressed: "I was glad to get off really," he said. "They scripted it all, and the script they gave us was so awful that we just said: 'fuck that,' and made up our own thing. We thought we were being really witty, and we were just met with this wall of nothing. But, of course, everyone was just looking around over their shoulders, seeing who was sitting behind them. Nobody gave a shit what was going on on stage. It was silly." "We went down like a bucket of cold sick," he concluded.

Although McGregor may not have been keen on self-promotion, others were only too happy to do it for him. In November 1997 he raced to number one in the British charts, when dance group PF Project sampled his voice from the *Trainspotting* soundtrack for their hit, "Choose Life"—although the first time McGregor heard it was in a Scarborough disco during the filming of *Little Voice*.

Away from the public eye, he also gave his support to the Marie Curie Cancer Care charity, and the Rachel House children's hospice in Fife.

By this time, Carol McGregor had given up her teaching

job to become Ewan's full-time personal assistant. She organised much of his busy schedule and dealt with the ever increasing amount of fan-mail, particularly from his growing female following in America. Carol also helped set up a new scheme to provide voice-overs on films for the blind. Her first project was *Shallow Grave*.

Management at Scotland's leading cinema for encouraging local talent and showing independent films, the Glasgow Film Theatre, were delighted when McGregor agreed to be their honorary patron. But in 1997, the actor became involved in a project that had far greater implications for the British film industry. He teamed up with his closest actor friends Jude Law, Sadie Frost, Jonny Lee Miller and Sean Pertwee, plus producers Damon Bryant and Bradley Adams, to form a new company. In December that year they launched Natural Nylon—their own $100 million production company, which aimed to challenge the traditional dominance of the Hollywood studios.

Frustrated at the lack of input and control they had over their work, Law, Bryant and American-based Richard Burns had originally set up Natural Nylon in 1995—the first word representing their attitude and the second an acronym of New York and London. The intention was that the company would enable them to control their own destinies, making international movies on their own terms.

Inspired by the founding principles of United Artists, a breakaway studio launched by the likes of Charlie Chaplin and Douglas Fairbanks eighty years earlier, McGregor and

Co. also wanted to use their rising status to create a solid production base in Britain that would stem the exodus of home-grown talent across the Atlantic.

Unlike Oldman, Roth and Day Lewis before them, the latest British stars were setting up a situation where Hollywood would come to them. And with the British film industry booming, there was never going to be a better time to do it. Miramax, a division of the Disney empire, which had backed a number of McGregor's previous projects, had already set up a London-based production house to cash in on the British boom.

The actors—all directors with equal shares in their new company—agreed to continue with other work, but pledged to devote a large chunk of their time to Nylon projects. Their first big announcement was suitably impressive. They had secured $100 million funding for 10 movies to be made primarily in Britain, although big American companies like Sony Pictures, Polygram Filmed Entertainment, Trademark and Alliance had all pledged financial backing. It was a remarkable breakthrough.

Some of the Nylon team were scheduled to star in the $23 million cyber thriller *eXistenZ*, directed by David Cronenburg, and also starring Jennifer Jason Leigh. Law was planning a movie about the poet Christopher Marlowe. There were also plans for a film about the life of The Beatles' manager Brian Epstein, an adaptation of Iain Banks' *The Bridge*, and a contemporary thriller based on the book *Psychoville*.

All five were said to have agreed to star in *The Hellfire*

Club, an £8 million movie about the debauched goings on in mid-18th-century British aristocratic society. McGregor was scheduled to play the politician John Wilkes, and in another part-Nylon production planned for mid-1998 he would play James Joyce in a film about the author's wife, Nora Barnacle.

McGregor had been committed to the part before Nylon were involved, and was keen to get going as soon as possible. "I've been reading up a lot about James Joyce," he said, "and he was such an incredible guy. I can't wait to try that out." But just where he was going to find the time was anyone's guess.

When he returned to work in Spring 1998, McGregor travelled to Montreal to begin filming the $15 million American independent movie *Eye of the Beholder.* Directed by Stephan Elliott, who had made *The Adventures of Priscilla, Queen of the Desert,* the film features McGregor as a hi-tech private eye who becomes obsessed with a mysterious woman, played by Ashley Judd, who he discovers is a serial killer. Singer k. d. lang also stars in the movie adapted from a novel by Marc Behm.

McGregor's next project was *Nora,* which would be filmed in Ireland. And in September 1998, he planned to put movies to one side and take a lead role in a stage play. The idea had come to him during the filming of *A Life Less Ordinary* in Utah at the end of 1996.

"I was depressed one night and I phoned up my uncle Denis," recalled McGregor. "He's a great ear for me. I said: 'I really want to do a play. I need to do a play before this idea is so frightening I'll never do it again, and I want you to direct it because I'm frightened enough about it, and I think it would be nice if you were there."

They chose a sixties farce, *Little Malcolm and His Struggle Against The Eunuchs*. It was to be staged at the Hampstead Theatre Club, just a short distance from his home in north London, with Ewan leading a young cast in a tale of rebellious art students who take action against college authorities when they are not allowed to express themselves through their work. If not entirely autobiographical, the play reflects aspects of his own life—the pupil who rebelled in school, and the student who detested the strict rules that denied him his chance at RADA.

"Last year he was talking to his uncle and he was saying how sad it was that his generation were labelled apathetic," said a friend. "Denis said that every generation of that age had always been labelled apathetic. They chose a play that goes against that, encapsulates his feeling against authority. It is something that is very close to his heart."

The uncle and nephew also planned to do a movie together at long last. *Don't Think Twice*, a comedy about a struggling rock 'n' roll band, was due to be filmed in the west of Scotland towards the end of the year.

Those were the definite projects. As if that was not enough, McGregor was also linked to a string of others. Macdonald and Boyle had scouted locations in Thailand for one of their next projects, a $15 million adaptation of Alex Garland's *The Beach*, and a part was earmarked for the acting member of their team. Meanwhile Boyle was also reported to be directing one instalment of a film in three parts, *Alien Love Triangle*. He offered his friend a part, but McGregor's schedule was already full, and Kenneth Branagh was chosen to lead the cast instead.

There was also speculation that McGregor was in the frame for the lead role in a film version of Iain Banks' psychological thriller, *Complicity*, and a starring role alongside George Clooney in a movie about prisoners from a Siberian labour camp who walked 4,000 miles to freedom. Even Yoko Ono reportedly wanted him to play John Lennon in a film about The Beatles. "I was glad to read about it in the newspapers," said McGregor. "That would be very nice but I don't know anything about it. But I would have to think about that one, because none of the other Beatles would want her to make the film, so I probably wouldn't do it."

At the beginning of 1998 a deluge of McGregor films were finally due to make it to the big screen. *Nightwatch*, which had been postponed several times, was finally released in America on April 17 to mixed reviews. The *San Francisco Chronicle* reviewer found it hard going: "It's rough when it works and rough when it doesn't. Much of the first hour is made up of slow patches, while the last 20 minutes are ugly and terrifying."

The team behind *The Serpent's Kiss* were also confident of finally securing a distribution deal, after the film received its British Premiere at the Scottish People's Film Festival in Glasgow in February. They blamed the lengthy delay on the complexities of arranging different deals in different countries.

In Britain *Velvet Goldmine*, one of the most eagerly anticipated movies of the year, was originally scheduled to open on April 17, although editing problems caused a delay which meant that its release was postponed until September 25, around the same time it would be released in America. *Rogue Trader* was also scheduled for release that month, and *The Rise and Fall of Little Voice* was planned for November. *Eye of the Beholder*, due for release in early 1999, would be the last McGregor offering before *Star Wars*—the biggest one of all— took on the world.

EPILOGUE

21ST CENTURY BOY

The actor peered through the bullet-proof windows of his limousine as it swept through the remote-controlled gates of his new London mansion. As usual, tourists weighed down by cameras were hanging around on the pavement. One of the celebrity bus tours that wheeled past his new home three times each day was just pulling up.

Everything had changed after the release of *Star Wars* almost a year earlier. Now, there seemed to be no escape from the constant media attention, the hangers-on, and the fans. Suddenly, he was mobbed everywhere he went. He couldn't remember the last time he had been able to visit his local pub. Most of the fans meant no harm, but they all wanted a piece of him, and their relentless attention was stripping away the last vestiges of the life he had once known. Inevitably, there were others with more sinister motives—some lunatic or other always seemed to be able to get hold of his ex-directory number, leaving threatening messages on his answering machine. Outside the 10-foot-high wall that shielded his home from the ever-present prying eyes, people routinely went through his bins, searching for anything they could use against him.

His world seemed to be shrinking, as he was increasingly forced to take refuge behind ever more elaborate security measures, intruder alarms and video surveillance.

The stream of advisers who had suddenly appeared in his life suggested the appointment of bodyguards, and an immediate move to a bigger home with even more advanced security measures. He had become an international superstar, but he was also the victim of his own success. In the back of his sleek new limousine, he sat back and sighed. It was May 2000. If this was the new millennium, he wanted out. . . .

This grim vision of the future may well be the nightmare scenario for the laid-back Ewan McGregor. He once spoke about how Hollywood seemed to be only about becoming famous, and wondered how much people were prepared to lose in order to achieve that dream.

McGregor had always said that Hollywood's version of stardom did not interest him, but, in reality, from the moment he accepted the role in *Star Wars*, it was no longer something he could ignore.

In Britain, McGregor had already become a icon for twenty-somethings, the embodiment of the "cool Britannia" image concocted by Tony Blair's spin doctors. But speculation about how his status would alter after *Star Wars* was something he seemed strangely reluctant to explore.

"I'm constantly being called upon to think about it by people asking me all the time," he said in February 1998. "But that seems to be of more interest to them. Y'know, I don't worry about it. If I had worried about it, I wouldn't have done the film. I have no idea what will happen next. To me, it's massive and it's *Star Wars*. It was more interesting to see how a film like that operates, and how a crew of five hundred people work together and stuff like that. There's no point worrying about it. What can I do? I don't know if people are going to start camping outside my house. They might, we'll see, and I'll get rid of them if they do."

But just how big did the actor think *Star Wars* would make him? Harrison Ford, for example, owed everything to the original films.

"Yeah, look what happened to him," he replied. "Look what happened to Mark Hamill, though!"

It was a typically incisive response, but he was not particularly interested in worrying about the potentially negative aspects of his success.

Whatever Ewan McGregor may have thought, in 1998 there seemed little doubt that, whether he liked it or not, *Star*

Wars would dramatically change his life. Parallels were drawn with the rise to prominence of Leonardo DiCaprio. Following the release of *Titanic*, and the extraordinary scenes of mass-hysteria wherever he appeared, DiCaprio joined the select band of actors who could command $20 million for one movie. *Daily Variety's* Mike Fleming believes *Star Wars* has the potential to be McGregor's *Titanic*.

"Nothing is ever sure in Hollywood," he said, "but if there was ever a movie you would lay your bets on to be a tremendous smash hit, it would be *Star Wars*. McGregor has the talent to go to the top. If he talks about purity of craft that's laudable. But let's face it, he is in what is going to be the biggest movie of that year bar none and he is probably going to be in three of the biggest movies of all time. If he doesn't realise that he should brace himself, because these are going to be monstrous.

"If I was trying to cast him and selling the slot that followed *Star Wars* I would be looking for a pretty big price hike for him. There is just no way that movie is not going to take. There is no way that this guy is not going to be an international box office star. He will be in everyone's faces and he will be a household name. Then it depends on the moves he makes subsequent to that. But it sounds to me like he has got the bases covered."

His director on *Brassed Off* and *Little Voice*, Mark Herman, warned that McGregor's success made his next move "dangerous", sentiments echoed by *The Guardian's* Derek Malcolm:

"No-one knows exactly how good he is. He's going to go into *Star Wars* and he will certainly be better than the puppets they normally use. Whether he'll ever show 50 per cent of his ability in a film like that, God knows. But he's got personality, power and he is good-looking enough to be a star.

"He's probably trying one big American epic. Whether he wants to try others afterwards I don't know. If it's very successful he may be forced to, because he may become very rich. I think he has got the best motives. The danger is that he will try and be a Hollywood star and find that is not quite what he wants to do in the end.

"It is very, very seductive getting well known throughout the world. I'm sure he enjoys that. I think he knows the score. Even so, if he is not careful I think there is a danger he will get drawn into it in the wrong way. He should be very careful to remain within his own culture, making films about his own culture, rather than becoming a big star in Hollywood and making crap, which is mostly what they do now. Ewan will probably say to himself, 'I'm going to do intelligent work if possible but if I'm asked to do a great big Hollywood epic for lots of money I will do that too.' I think he is progressing as an actor, but he still has his limits. I'm afraid if he goes into a lot of Hollywood movies those limits will be even more exposed."

Yet despite all the hype surrounding *Star Wars*, McGregor still maintained his commitment to British films, alongside a healthy scepticism of Hollywood:

"The work I'm doing here in Britain is more meaningful

and seems to be more about character and stories, as opposed to explosions," he said. "LA is only to make films, that is all there is there. And that is good when you are making a film. When you are not working, I don't know what [you] do, eat massive amounts of food the whole time. Here in this country we've got so much art and theatre, and music and really cool people. And you're always surrounded by stuff to feed off for your next part. There's so much there, and there's nothing like that in LA, except: 'How many cup-holders has your jeep got?' That's it. That's as far as you get. I would go there and make a film, and come back. But I would never go there and stay. I would just be bored."

And so it seems that, thus far at least, the boy from Crieff remains the same down-to-earth character who left school and set out to make his fortune in the movies. "His mum and I have been on the set of most of his films and the comment we always get is how nice he is," said Jim McGregor. "It doesn't matter if you're the guy who makes the tea or the director, Ewan chats and makes friends with everybody.

"We are so proud of him. It is very difficult to be subjective about how good Ewan is when he is your own son. But we always knew he had talent. Carol says she always knew he would be a star. It has [only] surprised us that it has happened so fast."

As McGregor flew out to North America to begin filming *Eye of the Beholder* in the final week of March 1998, he found himself in an extraordinarily privileged position for a young actor—with the choice of virtually any script he wanted, the respect of his peers, and a contented, comfortable family life.

"So when the lights go down and the curtains go up and it says Ewan McGregor, it's amazing. I look and I think: 'It's me.' Even when it's not very good it's great to see yourself up there. Those were my dreams, and there they are."

FILMOGRAPHY

BEING HUMAN
Warner Bros.
Director: Bill Forsyth
Co-star: Robin Williams
Character: Alvarez
Released US: 1994
US gross takings: $1.5 million

SHALLOW GRAVE
Figment Films/Channel Four Films
Director: Danny Boyle
Co-stars: Kerry Fox,
Christopher Eccleston
Character: Alex Law
Released UK: January 1995
UK gross takings: £5.1 million

BLUE JUICE
Skreba Films/Channel Four Films
Director: Carl Prechezer
Co-stars: Sean Pertwee, Catherine
Zeta Jones, Steven Mackintosh,
Peter Gunn
Character: Dean Raymond
Released UK: September 1995
UK gross takings: £256,375

TRAINSPOTTING
Figment Films/Channel Four Films
Director: Danny Boyle
Co-stars: Robert Carlyle, Jonny Lee
Miller, Ewen Bremner
Character: Mark Renton
Released UK: February 1996
UK gross takings: £12.4 million

EMMA
Haft Entertainment/Matchmaker
Films/Miramax Films
Director: Douglas McGrath
Co-stars: Gwyneth Paltrow,
Toni Collette, Alan Cumming,
Greta Scacchi
Character: Frank Churchill
Released UK: September 1996
UK gross takings: £5.2 million

BRASSED OFF
Channel Four Films/Miramax Films
Director: Mark Herman
Co-Stars: Pete Postlethwaite, Tara
Fitzgerald, Stephen Tompkinson
Character: Andy
Released UK: November 1996
UK gross takings: £3.4 million

THE PILLOW BOOK

Kasander and Wigman Productions

Director: Peter Greenaway

Co-stars: Vivian Wu, Yoshi Oida, Ken Ogata

Character: Jerome

Released UK: November 1996

UK gross takings: £507,425

A LIFE LESS ORDINARY

Figment Films

Director: Danny Boyle

Co-stars: Cameron Diaz, Holly Hunter, Delroy Lindo

Character: Robert

Released UK: October 1997

UK gross takings: £3.4 million

NIGHTWATCH

Dimension Films/Miramax Films

Director: Ole Bornedal

Co-stars: Nick Nolte, Patricia Arquette, Josh Brolin

Released US: April 1998

Character: Martin Belos

Information on film takings courtesy of Entertainment Data Inc.

SHORTS

FAMILY STYLE (1993)

Director: Justin Chadwick

SWIMMING WITH THE FISHES (1996)

Director: Justin Chadwick

TO BE RELEASED

VELVET GOLDMINE

Single Cell Pictures

Director: Todd Haynes

Co-stars: Christian Bale, Jonathan Rhys Myers, Toni Collette, Eddie Izzard

Character: Curt Wild

THE SERPENT'S KISS

Miramax Films

Director: Philippe Rousselot

Co-stars: Pete Postlethwaite, Richard E Grant, Greta Scacchi

Character: Meneer Chrome

ROGUE TRADER

Granada Films/David Paradine

Director: James Dearden

Co-star: Anna Friel

Character: Nick Leeson

Provisional UK release date: Autumn 1998

THE RISE AND FALL OF LITTLE VOICE

Miramax Films/Scala Productions

Director: Mark Herman

Co-stars: Jane Horrocks, Michael Caine, Jim Broadbent

Character: Billy

STAR WARS: EPISODE 1

Lucasfilm Ltd

Director: George Lucas

Co-stars: Liam Neeson, Samuel L Jackson, Natalie Portman

Character: Obi-Wan Kenobi

Provisional US release date: May 25, 1999

EYE OF THE BEHOLDER

Filmline International

Director: Stephan Elliott

Co-stars: Patrick Bergin, Jason Priestly, Geneviève Bujold, Ashley Judd, k. d. lang

Character: Private detective

In production Spring 1998, provisional release date: early 1999

TELEVISION

LIPSTICK ON YOUR COLLAR

Channel Four (1993)

Director: Renny Rye

Co-stars: Giles Thomas, Louise Germaine, Kimberley Huffman

Character: Private Mick Hopper

SCARLET AND BLACK

BBC (1993)

Director: Ben Bolt

Co-stars: Rachel Weisz, Alice Krige

Character: Julien Sorel

DOGGIN' AROUND

Ariel Productions for BBC (1994)

Producer: Otto Plaschkes

Co-star: Elliot Gould

Character: Tom Clayton

KAVANAGH QC

Episode: *Nothing But The Truth* (1995)

Central Films production for ITV

Producer: Chris Kelly

Co-stars: John Thaw, Geraldine James

Character: David Armstrong

TALES FROM THE CRYPT

Episode: *Cold War* (1996)

HBO

Director: Andy Morahan

Co-star: Jane Horrocks

Character: Ford

KARAOKE

BBC/Channel Four (1996)

Director: Renny Rye

Co-stars: Albert Finney, Richard E Grant, Julie Christie, Keeley Hawes

Character: Young Man

ER

Episode: *The Long Way Around* (1997)

NBC

Director: Christopher Chulak

Co-stars: Julianna Margulies, George Clooney, Currie Graham

Character: Duncan

AWARDS

EMPIRE AWARDS 1996

Best Actor

VARIETY CLUB OF GREAT BRITAIN AWARDS 1997

Best Actor for *Trainspotting*

LONDON CRITICS' CIRCLE FILM AWARDS 1997

Best Actor for *Trainspotting*, *Brassed Off* and *Emma*

BAFTA SCOTLAND 1997

Best Actor for *Trainspotting*

GUILD OF REGIONAL FILM WRITERS 1997

Robert Shelton Award for outstanding contribution to the British Film Industry

EVENING STANDARD AWARDS 1997

Best Actor

SCOTTISH PEOPLE'S FILM FESTIVAL 1997

Best Actor

BRITISH FILM INSTITUTE 1997

Actor of the year—award shared with Sir Ian McKellen

EMPIRE AWARDS 1997

Best Actor

EMPIRE AWARDS 1998

Best Actor

NOMINATIONS

MTV MOVIE AWARDS 1997

Best Breakthrough Performance nomination for *Trainspotting*

EMMY AWARDS 1997

Best Dramatic Performance by a Guest Actor nominaton for *ER*

MTV MOVIE AWARDS 1998

Best Dance Sequence nomination, with Cameron Diaz, for *A Life Less Ordinary*

REFERENCES

CHAPTER I

"Mrs Lawson was always elegant in the dancing" from BA interview with Rev Sandy Tait, November 1997.

"Performing the tango" from BA interview with Rev Sandy Tait, November 1997.

"I was the world's worst carpet salesman" *The Scotsman* 3 January 1998.

"People tended to give the impression" from BA interview with Councillor Ian Hunter.

"He left because he was fed up with everybody" *The Scotsman* 13 October 1997.

"I knew he would go up The Knock" *The Scotsman* 13 October 1997.

CHAPTER II

"It's fair to say we stood out" and following, from BA interview with Iain King, November 1997.

"We were being taught Latin" from BA interview with Iain King, November 1997.

"He was a great guy" from BA interview with Fergus Adams, November 1997.

"Ewan was confident, happy and joined in" and following, from BA interview with Jane Kennedy, November 1997.

"I didn't hate school. I just didn't get it" *The Scotsman* 13 October 1997.

"Incredible desire to be loved and wanted" *Neon* October 1997.

"Went off the rails" *The Mirror* 15 November 1997.

"I didn't realise it at the time" *The Times* 13 October 1997.

"I had a great love for music and art" and following, *Parkinson* BBC TV February 1998.

"She was a Jean Brodie type" *The Times* 13 October 1997.

"Was perhaps starting to get embarrassing for my father" *Film Review* November 1997.

"I felt I had something to live up to" and following, *The Face* November 1996.

"An arrangement of the 18th-
century sea-song"
The Morrisonian June 1988.

"Ewan couldn't compete with his
brother" *Scottish Daily Mail*
14 January 1997.

"I think there was a period when
he was unhappy" and following,
The Scotsman 13 October 1997.

"She was right, and it was a really
brave decision"
UK Premiere March 1996.

"They didn't make me feel bad"
The Mirror 15 November 1997.

"I don't regret it at all, no. What
I do regret" *The Morrisonian*
February 1997.

CHAPTER III

"You get out of there at sixteen"
Parkinson BBC TV February 1998.

"From the moment he could walk"
Scottish Daily Mail 14 January 1997.

"My experience of children and
acting" from BA interview with
Rev Sandy Tait, November 1997.

"We got a call from the minister to
say there was a problem" and
following, *Daily Record*
31 January 1997.

"There were a lot of lines and the
minister" *The Scotsman*
13 October 1997.

"I can't remember how Ewan" from
BA interview with Rev Sandy Tait,
November 1997.

"The play went well enough" from
BA interview with Rev Sandy Tait,
November 1997.

"She said Ewan had just got his
first big break" from BA interview
with Rev Sandy Tait,
November 1997.

"He gave people flowers"
Parkinson BBC TV February 1998.

"We would always go out as a
family when Denis came home"
Scottish Daily Mail 14 January 1997.

"I walked in front of a procession"
and following, from BA interview
with Colin Mayell, January 1998.

"My attic was full of the figures"
and following, from BA interview
with Alastair Maclachlan,
November 1997.

"It all became about legs and I fell
in love" *Empire* November 1997.

"One of us would be Olivia"
Neon October 1997.

"The SAS would be proud"
Neon October 1997.

"We got up to a lot of mischief"
The Scotsman 13 October 1997.

"It was intended as a bit of a joke"
and following, from BA interview
with Yvonne McIldowie, November
1997.

"We did a revue to mark the 125th
anniversary" and following, from
BA interview with Alastair
Maclachlan, November 1997.

"To take us to Hollywood"
The Morrisonian June 1988.

"Despite an excessive wig"
The Morrisonian June 1988.

CHAPTER IV

"You know, 'Someone's having an affair' " *UK Premiere* March 1996.

"Suddenly I was where I wanted to be" *The Mirror* 15 November 1997.

"Arsehole" *UK Premiere* January 1997.

"Ewan was a good laugh" and following, from BA interview with Ian Grieve, November 1997.

"We did lots of workshops" and following, from BA interview with Liz Carruthers, November 1997.

"I loved Crieff. But it's the kind of place" *UK Premiere* March 1996.

"From the minute he walked in the door" *Scottish Daily Mail* 14 January 1997.

"It was a hard year. I had to do everything" *The Mirror* 15 November 1997.

"We were all thrown in at the deep end" from BA interview with Paul Kininmonth, December 1997.

"Ewan's speeches passed" from BA interview with Maggie McMillan, November 1997.

"I knew what they were planning" from BA interview with Rhonda Stephen, November 1997.

"I realised this was exactly what I wanted to do" *The Face* November 1996.

"He said that up until the year at Kirkcaldy" *Scottish Daily Mail* 14 January 1997.

CHAPTER V

"I'm sure he kissed Mary" from BA interview with Alastair Maclachlan, November 1997.

"I honestly can't remember" from BA interview with Mary Green, November 1997.

"I think we started going out together" and following, from BA interview with Vicky Grant (née McNally), November 1997.

"I just hadn't done it" *Neon* October 1997.

"Ewan was a great guy" and following, from BA interview with Paul Kininmonth, November 1997.

"Ewan was open enough" and following, from BA interview with Paul Kininmonth, November 1997.

"They were very, very together" from BA interview with Paul Kininmonth, December 1997.

"There was a bit of a bust up" from BA interview with Paul Kininmonth, December 1997.

"Listen lads" and following, from BA interview with Tom Lawrence, November 1997.

"Drama patients" and following, from BA interview with Tom Lawrence, November 1997.

"I remember they both" and following, from BA interview with Tom Lawrence, November 1997.

"At the end, I remember Ewan gave me a big hug" from BA interview with Paul Kininmonth, December 1997.

CHAPTER VI

"This is great, this is the first time I've ever got my own back on RADA" *Parkinson* BBC TV February 1998.

"You need to weed out at that stage" and following, from BA interview with Kenneth Rea, February 1998.

"Those who get in" from BA interview with Kenneth Rea, February 1998.

"It was just a summer job" from BA interview with Paolo Diotaiuti, November 1997.

"That boosted my confidence" *The Herald* 2 March 1993.

"I tell them that although we will give them skills" from BA interview with Kenneth Rea, February 1998.

"I didn't seem to have any" *Neon* October 1997.

"I always thought I was fantastic until I got to drama school" *The Face* November 1996.

"There are things you are taught at drama school" from BA interview with Kenneth Rea, February 1998.

"Some of them are away from home" from BA interview with Kenneth Rea, February 1998.

"It took me at least four years to get rid of the garbage" *Evening Standard* 10 September 1997.

"I liked it there" *Scottish Daily Mail* 15 January 1997.

"Now it just annoys me" *Neon* October 1997.

"I came off and thought, 'Fuck, that's it, I've blown it' " *UK Premiere* March 1996.

"A lot of casting" from BA interview with Kenneth Rea, February 1998.

CHAPTER VII

"We had been told he was wonderful" and following, from BA interview with Rosemarie Whitman, January 1998.

"He was very scruffy" from BA interview with Sally Jay, November 1997.

"Doing him was extraordinarily easy" *The Herald* 2 March 1993.

"When his parents came to the set" from BA interview with Sally Jay, November 1997.

"He was remarkable" from BA interview with Rosemarie Whitman, January 1998.

"He'd talk to me and warn me about what might happen after Lipstick came out" *Neon* October 1997.

"I think he is a genius"
The Herald 2 March 1993.

"I was so proud" and following,
from BA interview with Rosemarie
Whitman, January 1998.

"We knew nothing about him"
The Times 27 March 1993.

"I dealt with it really badly"
UK Premiere March 1996.

"I was waiting for six months for it
to come out" *Neon* October 1997.

"It was funny to see him when he
gets up on the desk in a gold suit"
Daily Record 31 January 1997.

"We've had Ewan in" from BA
interview with Ros Wolfes,
December 1997.

"It was completely different" from
BA interview with Ros Wolfes,
December 1997.

CHAPTER VIII

"I felt terrible" and following, from
BA interview with Ros Wolfes,
December 1997.

"I am very ambitious. I always
wanted to be an actor"
Today 2 November 1993.

"It was Christmas time" from BA
interview with Ros Wolfes,
December 1997.

"Two weeks into that and I was
moping" *Calgary Sun*
5 August 1996.

"I had to do two streaks across the
stage" *Daily Mirror* 30 October 1993.

"Ewan gets guillotined" *New
Woman* April 1998.

"One day I was naked the whole
time" *Daily Mirror* 30 October 1993.

"I persuaded him. I went on"
The People 31 October 1993.

"I see you dress to the right"
Neon October 1997.

"There were a lot of nude scenes"
Daily Mirror 30 October 1993.

"I had a complete crisis"
Mail on Sunday 31 October 1993.

"Once I put on my military uniform
and we started filming"
Daily Record 30 October 1993.

"Ewan McGregor isn't the slight,
pallid figure of the novel"
The Independent 1 November 1993.

"It may be argued"
Daily Mail 1 November 1993.

"McGregor could have beefed up
his role" *Daily Mirror*
1 November 1993.

"As Julien, Ewan McGregor is
simply" *The Sunday Times*
7 November 1993.

"The performance by Ewan seemed
short on stamina"
Sunday Mirror 7 November 1993.

"Ewan fell madly in love" and
following from BA interview with
Ros Wolfes, December 1997.

"Immediate attraction"
Daily Mirror 30 October 1993.

"I'm a romantic person"
Daily Mirror 30 October 1993.

"It's providing me with"
Mail on Sunday 31 October 1993.

"She's tiny as well so it must have looked very funny"
Daily Mirror 30 October 1993.

"I don't envisage marriage and babies" *The People*
14 November 1993.

"I got a phone call one day" from BA interview with Ros Wolfes, December 1997.

CHAPTER IX

"I just realised after writing about ten pages" *2nd Opinion*
Summer 1996.

"Had I never met Andrew"
The Telegraph Magazine
27 September 1997.

"When I read it I thought it was a really exciting script"
Sight and Sound January 1995.

"Andrew didn't want someone like" *UK Premiere* November 1997.

"Before I produced Shallow Grave"
The Guardian 12 January 1995.

"We all agreed that the script was the bible" *The Guardian* 12 January 1995.

"We stayed in a flat"
Daily Mirror 19 January 1995.

"Ooh, it's me" *Time Out* June 1997.

"It was brilliant" *Time Out* June 1997.

"Don't be ridiculous"
Empire January 1995.

CHAPTER X

"Clammed up like a venus fly trap" and following *Sunday Mail*
7 November 1993.

"The things that went on there"
The Times 13 October 1997.

"I wasn't satisfied with it any more" *The Times* 13 October 1997.

"They're difficult. I like difficult women" *The Times* 13 October 1997.

"My sister has a great facility for languages" and following, from Lesley Hussell interview with Marianne Mavrakis, January 1997.

"I knew from the first day I saw her" *The Mirror* 15 November 1997.

"She told me he was an actor" and following, Lesley Hussell interview with Marianne Mavrakis, January 1997.

"All I said was 'Oui' "
The Virginian-Pilot 23 October 1997.

"It was a wonderful wedding" and following, *Scottish Daily Mail*
15 January 1997.

"Dad I completely forgot"
Scottish Daily Mail 15 January 1997.

"We all cooked for each other at night" *The Face* November 1996.

"They were very discreet"
from BA interview with Chris Kelly, December 1997.

"My future wife was sitting upstairs" *US Intervue*
November 1997.

"He had to be this adorable young man" from BA interview with Chris Kelly, December 1997.

"They did this massively long scene" from BA interview with Chris Kelly, December 1997.

"Ewan McGregor and I came down" *Empire* August 1996.

"I remember Ewan was under the weather" from BA interview with Peter Salmi, December 1997.

"A couple of guys down there" from BA interview with Peter Salmi, December 1997.

"I had a great time, filming in Cornwall" *Details* November 1997.

"It's a bit muddled in the middle" *Details* November 1997.

"We bit off" from BA interview with Peter Salmi, December 1997.

"When she came down" from BA interview with Peter Salmi, December 1997.

CHAPTER XI

"God, did we really shoot this film" *The New York Times* 1 June 1997.

"Love, trust, friendship" *The Herald* 14 January 1995.

"I liked this from the start" *The Sunday Times* 8 May 1994.

"Tar-black comedy" *Variety* January 1995.

"Hitchcock would have admired its ruthlessness" *The Observer* 8 January 1995.

"I think the film looks like an $8 million movie" *The Sunday Times* 18 December 1994.

"Pretty, but pretty unconvincing" *The Herald* 7 January 1995.

"They seem to analyse things more than we do" *Scotland on Sunday* 16 April 1995.

"We never expected it" *Sight and Sound* January 1995.

"A lot of the album is about Jarvis Cocker's experiences" quoted by Monika Maurer in *The Richmond Review* 1996.

"They're writing pop songs" *The Richmond Review* 1996.

"I've spent a lot of my career building up plausible characters" *Sight and Sound* January 1995.

"We're not up on a hill waiting for the masses to arrive" *The Richmond Review* 1996.

"We're not making films for the critics" *2nd Opinion* Summer 1996.

"We've been taken out to lunch by Disney" *Empire* January 1995.

"What I want to do" *Empire* January 1995.

"Hollywood wants to control individuals" *Festival Films Website, 1996.*

"Fuck all" *The Richmond Review* 1996.

"The idea right from the beginning" *UK Premiere* March 1996.

"You've got to be ruthless" *2nd Opinion* Summer 1996.

"If you're going to compare us to the book" *The Richmond Review* 1996.

"One of the great things about the book" *2nd Opinion* Summer 1996.

"We were the only people who could get *Trainspotting* made" *Neon* February 1998.

"Those bastards. They gave me the script" *The Mirror* 15 November 1997.

"I only found this out recently" *Empire* November 1997.

"Ewan was a logical choice" *Neon* February 1998.

"A million birthday presents" *Parkinson* BBC TV February 1998.

CHAPTER XII

"There's aw these punters runnin' aroond like blue-arsed flies" *Scotland on Sunday* 11 February 1996.

"Ewan is normally quite a chunky guy" *Neon* February 1998.

"I felt really good that way" *The Observer* 15 June 1997.

"That was just something that had to be done" *The Irish Times* 21 June 1997.

"We didn't really do any drugs" *Paper Magazine* July 1996.

"I felt these characters were part" *Neon* February 1998.

"I just watched them from a distance" *The Independent on Sunday* 28 January 1996.

"These guys are fanatical" *The Guardian* 23 January 1996.

"I'd never heard anything like it" *Daily Record* 9 February 1996.

"To meet them you get that feeling" *Neon* February 1998.

"The hit had gone" *The Independent* 10 February 1996.

"He came round and he marked us all" *Neon* February 1998.

"It is my arm but moulded prosthetically" *The Independent on Sunday* 28 January 1996.

"I don't want to do it" *Neon* February 1998.

"The book is very clear about what it would be like" *The Guardian* 23 January 1996.

"A disgusting little film" *Daily Mail* 23 February 1996.

"*Trainspotting* pours scorn" *Daily Mail* 23 February 1996.

"In style, structure and subversive imagination" *Evening Standard* 22 February 1996.

"Juvenile, inane, puerile" *The Herald* 17 February 1996.

"Very realistically filmed" and following, *The Herald* 17 February 1996.

"Hearing how low these hard men" *Paper Magazine* July 1996.

"I thought about actually taking heroin" *Neon* February 1998.

"All the traditional information about heroin is there" *The Richmond Review* 1996.

"In the end it conforms" *Neon* February 1998.

"Some people will have you believe" *Scotland on Sunday* 4 February 1996.

"Five people shooting up heroin" quoted by Sylvia Paterson in *The Face* November 1996.

"This is the way it is" *Scotland on Sunday* 11 February 1996.

"I'm sick to death" *The List* July 1997.

"It does worry me that the characters have become heroes" *Neon* February 1998.

"We concentrated on the first 20 minutes" *The Sunday Times* 26 May 1996.

"For those of you who missed it" *The Mirror* 15 November 1997.

"I've met loads of Begbies in my time" *Neon* February 1998.

"How about we don't talk about Trainspotting at all" *The Face* November 1996.

"It's a nightmare of a drug" and following, *Parkinson* BBC TV February 1998.

"I will never forget" Scottish People's Film Festival (SPFF) February 1998.

CHAPTER XIII

"McGregor and Carlyle inhabit a much more successful industry" from BA interview with Derek Malcolm, December 1997.

"It has been a pretty amazing year for us" *Empire* December 1996.

"Fucking brilliant year" *Empire* December 1996.

"It was unlike anything I've done before" *The Pillow Book Official Website*.

"Greenaway really is an artist" *Time Out* October 1996.

"Then you find out he really didn't bother to write any" *Time Out* October 1996.

"I'm naked a lot of the time" *Buzz* March 1997.

"Do you honestly think" and following, *Neon* October 1997.

"Slightly embarrassing for the first second" *Time Out* 9 October 1996.

"I actually enjoyed it" *Entertainment Weekly* 15 June 1997.

"It's not easy for her to see things like that" *E! Online* October 1997.

"I'm glad to see you've inherited one of my major assets" *Details* November 1997.

"There's two schools on this one"
Neon October 1997.

"McGregor shows that he is"
Time Magazine 10 March 1997.

"One minute I was lying on the
floor" *The Independent on Sunday*
28 January 1996.

"Go to tea parties just to listen"
The Independent 20 August 1996.

"The most elegant actress"
Time Magazine 29 July 1996.

"McGregor looks more like the
man" *The Herald* 12 September 1996.

"*Emma* is an example" from BA
interview with Chris Kelly,
December 1997.

"My only reservation is that he
can't play period" from BA
interview with Otto Plaschkes,
December 1997.

"I never read the novel"
The Virginian-Pilot 23 October 1997.

"I think the film's all right but I
was so crap" *Time Out*
9 October 1996.

"It was more mates than passion"
Sky International December 1996.

"People got fed up with that
bunch" *E! Online* October 1997.

"I saw three-bedroomed houses
for sale" *Scotland on Sunday*
15 September 1996.

CHAPTER XIV

"Pale, slightly puffy face"
UK Premiere March 1996.

"I'm falling to bits"
UK Premiere March 1996.

"I wasn't prepared to be frightened" *The Face* November 1996.

"I phoned a lot of people, crying
down the phone"
The Times 13 October 1997.

"It's pretty common knowledge"
Calgary Sun 26 October 1997.

"I'm drunk so often" *The Face*
October 1997.

"I think differences work out"
The Virginian-Pilot 23 October 1997.

"The best thing about the year"
Channel 4 News 19 December 1997.

"I don't live the rock 'n' roll life"
The Mirror 15 November 1997.

"There are a lot of wrecked
marriages in this business"
Calgary Sun 5 August 1996.

"Our Mum goes to see Ewan, Eve
and the baby" and following, from
Lesley Hussell interview with
Marianne Mavrakis, January 1997.

"I'm lucky my family comes with
me wherever I go" *Sydney Morning
Herald* 13 December 1996.

"I don't think I have ever seen such
a devoted father" *The Mirror*
15 November 1997.

"How did fatherhood change you?"
and following, *Miami Herald*
24 October 1997.

"That's disgusting actually, isn't it?"
Empire November 1997.

"I'm private in terms of my family"
U Magazine November 1997.

"They don't necessarily have a big
party" from Lesley Hussell
interview with Marianne Mavrakis,
January 1997.

"None of your business"
The Times 13 October 1997.

"Being interviewed by an English
journalist" *The Independent on
Sunday* 9 November 1997.

"Dribbling" *The Face*
November 1996.

"People will do anything, it seems,
to be a big movie star"
Premiere March 1996.

"Hero? A symbol of our times
perhaps" *The Mirror* 15 November
1997.

"It's like asking, do you think of
yourself as a sexy person"
Empire November 1997.

"Cute looks and sexy Scottish
accent" *Glamour* April 1998.

"Simply because it's Ewan-Call-Me-
Sex-God-McGregor"
Company April 1998.

"The thing that surprises my fans
most about me" *Toronto Sun*
18 October 1997.

"Who's going to know who I am?"
Sky Magazine November 1997.

"He goes for quality scripts" from
Lesley Hussell interview with
Marianne Mavrakis, January 1997.

"When I met with agents in LA,
they would tell me" *Entertainment
Weekly* 13 June 1997.

CHAPTER XV

"Ole Bornedal, in remaking his own
art house hit" G. Allen Johnson,
San Francisco Examiner 17 April 1998.

"The performances were terrible
across the board" Shane Ham,
Journal X 17 April 1998.

"Maybe it's a great film in
Denmark" Shane Ham,
Journal X 17 April 1998.

"I don't like the way the business is
run" *U Magazine* November 1997.

"We have got really good writers
here" *Parkinson* BBC TV February
1998.

"Channel 4 saved the British film
industry" from BA interview with
Derek Malcolm, December 1997.

"I said in effect, Fuck America"
Neon October 1997.

"Ewan is an actor who's
potential has yet to be fulfilled"
and following, from BA interview
with Derek Malcolm, December
1997.

"I've always thought you could
have it both ways"
The Guardian 13 September 1996.

"So they can put on their poster"
UK Premiere March 1996.

"He's totally hot" *The Sunday Times*
15 December 1996.

"It's all there for him, if he wants it" *Time Out* October 1996.

"I don't know what I'd do if I wasn't working in LA" *Scotland on Sunday* 15 September 1996.

"One thing is certain, I'll never live in LA" *The Virginian-Pilot* 23 October 1997.

"It was a very relaxed shoot" and following, from BA interview with Robert Jones, January 1998.

"I'm passionate about it" *The Irish Times* 21 June 1997.

"Astonishingly grounded" *The Guardian* 13 September 1996.

"The first time I saw him" and following, from BA interview with Robert Jones, January 1998.

"Weird loyalty thing" *The Face* November 1996.

"Fucking bastards. Why didn't they fucking notice this" *The Face* November 1996.

CHAPTER XVI

"After a few meetings, Danny and I realised" *A Life Less Ordinary Official Website.*

"We sent them the script, told them Danny was director" *The Telegraph Magazine* 27 September 1997.

"McGregor's American accent wobbles in and out" Mick LaSalle, *San Francisco Chronicle* 17 April 1998.

"Had to use every ounce of his limited talent" Shane Ham, *Journal X* 17 April 1998.

"As soon as she walked into the room I knew she was right" *A Life Less Ordinary Official Website.*

"We've got to offer it to her. Now!" *A Life Less Ordinary Official Website.*

"Oh my God. She's just a fantastic woman, so brilliant" *UniverCity Magazine* October 1997.

"I didn't know the chemistry would be there between us, but it was" *US Interveu* November 1997.

"Let's talk about" and following, *Neon* October 1997.

"In the film I fall in love with Ewan's character" *Daily Record* 26 June 1997.

"Within minutes they've turned into the equivalent of a young married couple" *The Face* October 1997.

"There were a few in the original script" *Sunday Mail* 28 September 1997.

"It's very nice to kiss Cameron Diaz" *UniverCity Magazine* October 1997.

"We'd all go out and get fucking plastered" *The Face* October 1997.

"Being a doctor is more interesting than writing scripts" *Daily Record* 29 September 1997.

"He is something special. He'll soon get offers" *The Telegraph Magazine* 27 September 1997.

"He's the best there is, that's it. I've never felt happier" *U Magazine* November 1997.

"I would turn down any of these bloomin' multi-million pound things" *The Virginian-Pilot* 23 October 1997.

"I don't know what it is about Danny Boyle" SPFF February 1998.

"Ewan's a mate. He's also the best film actor in Britain at the moment" *Toronto Sun* 18 October 1997.

"He has got that thing Tom Hanks has" *Buzz* March 1997.

"It's not understood that I'll do all their films" *US Intervue* November 1997.

"How many has De Niro done with Scorsese?" *UK Premiere* November 1997.

"The weirdest fucking people I've ever met" *The Face* October 1997.

"I've got a black woollen hat with 'Pervert' written on the front" *The List* July 1997.

"I got fed up. You know, I got carded for buying cigarettes" *U Magazine* November 1997.

"I don't want to offend all the burghers of Salt Lake City" *E! Online* October 1997.

"I've been quoted as saying the most awful things about Utah" *US Intervue* November 1997.

"I did ER because I really like ER" *The Independent* 28 March 1997.

"They are great people. They've been doing it for three years together" *The Morrisonian* February 1997.

"It was a really shrewd move to put him in a show like ER" from BA interview with Mike Fleming, February 1998.

CHAPTER XVII

"I couldn't do anything because I was on set" and following, SPFF February 1998.

"What was so interesting about that time" *Los Angeles Times* 27 July 1997.

"In that scene I come offstage and he's in the wings" and following, *Toronto Sun* 18 October 1997.

"I was mad when I was doing it" *Neon* October 1997.

"What the hell am I doing?" *Neon* October 1997.

"I watched a lot of Iggy Pop" *Los Angeles Times* 27 July 1997.

"It's the idea of standing there in front of all those thousands of people" *Sky Magazine* November 1997.

"I wanted to know what it felt like to wear super-tight skinny little tops" *Los Angeles Times* 27 July 1997.

"It's really annoying music" *Los Angeles Times* 27 July 1997.

"I was like a schoolgirl, sitting in their dressing room" *US Intervue* November 1997.

"First instincts are usually best"
Official Star Wars Prequels Website.

"It felt pretty amazing"
U Magazine November 1997.

"I told my wife, because 'fuck them, I'm telling my wife' "
U Magazine November 1997.

"Copyright Lucasfilm"
Garry Jenkins *Empire Building*,
Citadel Press.

"I don't really like big blockbuster films" SPFF February 1998.

"When you're my age, and you were out there cheering" *Total Film* October 1997.

CHAPTER XVIII

"There was a theory apparently"
The Scotsman 3 January 1998.

"They just freaked" *The Scotsman* 3 January 1998.

"They are fantastic films" SPFF February 1998.

"Denis helped me with my audition speeches" *Daily Record* 21 February 1998.

"Ewan is a different personality to me" *Daily Record* 21 February 1998.

"A little bit odd" SPFF February 1998.

"He came up and sat with me"
Allentown Morning Call October 1997.

"We wrap it all up with confidentiality" from BA interview with David Brown, February 1998.

"It was a very, very big storm" and following, from BA interview with David Brown, February 1998.

"I walked into the props room"
UniverCity Magazine October 1997.

"Bloody lethal" *Total Film* October 1997.

"There's nothing cooler than being a Jedi Knight" *The Face* October 1997.

"The first day I got dressed properly it was quite a moment"
The Times 13 October 1997.

"There are 18 months of post-production" SPFF Februaury 1998.

"Just getting down to it" *Details* November 1997.

"It was so, so complex" SPFF February 1998.

"The exciting thing will be seeing it in the preview theatre" SPFF February 1998.

"It is amazing" and following from BA interview with David Brown, February 1998.

"Sir Alec has done some of the most incredible cinematic acting" SPFF February 1998.

"I've played harder parts. Alec Guinness was asked about acting in *Star Wars*"
Miami Herald 24 October 1997.

CHAPTER XIX

"You can't deny it's quite nice'
SPFF February 1998.

"There is this scene when I'm
crossing the street bringing
Cameron groceries"
Toronto Sun 18 October 1997.

"What a title, the best of the year"
The Sunday Times 26 October 1997.

"This is muddle in the guise of
marvel" *Independent on Sunday*
26 October 1997.

"I think it was inevitable" *Ireland
Film and Television Net Website.*

"Ewan was brilliant" from BA
interview with Elisabeth Karlsen,
February 1998.

"I would have been embarrassed.
What would I say?" *The Daily
Telegraph* 7 February 1998.

"I don't want to have any opinion
about him" *US Intervue* November
1997.

"We are male and female versions"
The List March 1998.

"Ewan is the best"
The List March 1998.

"She is a human dynamo"
Daily Record 21 February 1998.

"I'm still fractious when I get a bit
of time on my hands" *Daily Record*
21 February 1998.

"I really should take a holiday"
*Ireland Film and Television Net
Website.*

"I was glad to get off really"
U Magazine November 1997.

"We went down like a bucket of
cold sick" *The Face* December 1997.

"I've been reading up a lot about
James Joyce" *Ireland Film and
Television Net Website.*

"I was depressed one night and I
phoned up my uncle Denis"
UniverCity Magazine October 1997.

"I was glad to read about it in the
newspapers" *US Intervue*
November 1997.

"It's rough when it works and
rough when it doesn't"
Mick LaSalle, *San Francisco Chronicle*
17 April 1998

EPILOGUE

"I'm constantly being called upon"
SPFF February 1998.

"Yeah, look what happened to him"
SPFF February 1998.

"Nothing is ever sure" From BA
interview with Mike Fleming,
February 1998.

"No-one knows exactly" from BA
interview with Derek Malcolm,
December 1997.

"The work I'm doing here in
Britain" SPFF February 1998.

"His mum and I have been on the
set" *Daily Record* 31 January 1997.

"So when the lights go down"
SPFF February 1998.

PICTURE CREDITS

i. Ewan McGregor at Cannes
Famous Pictures & Features Agency
(Photo: Kurt Krieger)

iv. *Shallow Grave* Cast members
The Kobal Collection
(Photo: Nigel Robertson)

Blue Juice Cast members
The Ronald Grant Archive

v. Ewan McGregor in *Emma*
Aquarius Picture Library

vi & vii. McGregor, Macdonald,
Boyle & Hodge
Shoot (Photo: Adrian Green)

viii. *Trainspotting*: Bremner,
McGregor, Carlyle
All Action Pictures

Trainspotting: Worst Toilet
Aquarius Picture Library

ix. *Star Wars* Premiere
PA News (Photo: Rebecca Naden)

x. *Rogue Trader*
Popperfoto (Photo: Reuters)

A Life Less Ordinary
Aquarius Picture Library

xi. McGregor & Diaz, MTV Awards
All Action Pictures
(Photo: Paul Smith)

xii. Eve, Clara & Ewan at Cannes
Photo: Alan Davidson

Charity football match
Daily Record

SPFF Awards—*Daily Record*

xiii. Ewan McGregor & Denis
Lawson—*Daily Record*

Ewan & Family—*The Herald*
Picture Archive

xiv. *The Pillow Book*
The Ronald Grant Archive
(Photo: Marc Guillamot)

Brassed Off
The Ronald Grant Archive

xv. *Velvet Goldmine*
Aquarius Picture Library

xvi. Ducati launch, Brands Hatch
Rex Features Ltd
(Photo: Jim Bennett)

Ewan & fans, Glasgow 1998
Daily Record

INDEX